ALASKA:
Indians, Eskimos, Russians, and the Rest ❖❖❖❖

ALASKA:
Indians, Eskimos, Russians, and the Rest

CORA CHENEY

ILLUSTRATED WITH PHOTOGRAPHS AND MAPS

DODD, MEAD & COMPANY
New York

ILLUSTRATIONS COURTESY OF:

Alaska Historical Library, 17, 52, 53, 57, 60 *top*, 63, 73, 81, 87, 88, 91, 95, 99, 111, 112, 121, 132; Alaska State Museum, 18, 43, 48, 60 *bottom*, 61, 65, 68, 76, 82, 83, 84 *left*; Cora Cheney, 125; Naval Arctic Research Laboratory, Ben Partridge photo, 75; Sitka National Historical Park, 84 *right*.

All other photographs are by Ben Partridge.

The maps on pages 10, 30–31, and 134 are by Mary Denham Partridge.

1 2 3 4 5 6 7 8 9 10

Library of Congress Cataloging in Publication Data

Cheney, Cora.
   Alaska: Indians, Eskimos, Russians, and the rest.

   Includes index.
   SUMMARY: A history of Alaska from the arrival of its
native peoples to the building of the oil pipeline in the
1970's, with special emphasis on its Russian period.
   1. Alaska—History—Juvenile literature.
[1. Alaska—History] I. Title.
F904.3.C45   979.8   79–6638
ISBN 0–396–07792–7

For Jeanie Partridge
with love, from her true friend
Cora Cheney

Contents

ALASKA:

Indians, Eskimos, Russians, and the Rest ❖❖❖❖❖

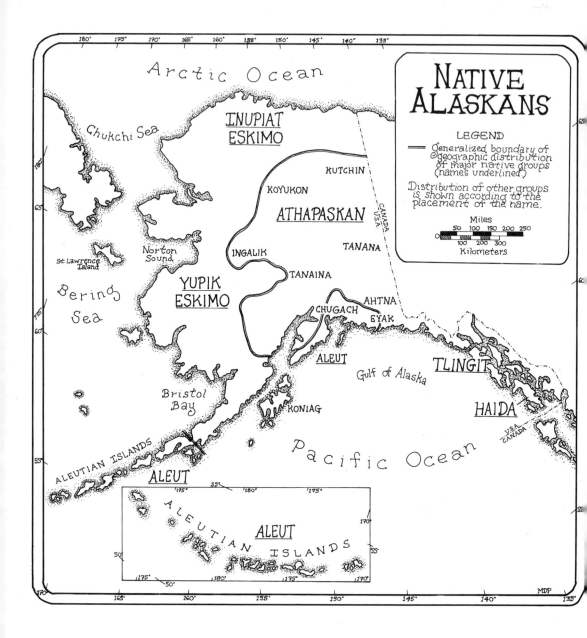

1 ❖❖❖

Alaska's First People

RAVEN squawked when he saw the saber-toothed tiger crouched behind a rock, its sleek body merging into the moist dark earth. The tiger's sharp, long upper teeth gleamed in the misty air as it watched the boy hunter with the stone weapon.

With a great catlike flash the animal leaped at the boy, but the boy had heard Raven's warning and escaped from the tiger. Later the tiger was killed by a mastodon, and the boy, grown to manhood, was drowned in a flood. That moment, shared by the boy, the tiger, and Raven, occurred twenty thousand years ago, near the present State of Alaska.

Today there are no more saber-toothed tigers, in Alaska or the whole world. And no more mastodons either, for that matter. But Raven is still in Alaska, and so are boys—Indian, Eskimo, Aleut, as well as a lot of latecomers.

Who were Alaska's first people? Where did they come from, and when? Perhaps thirty to forty thousand years ago, the first human beings to reach the American continents entered by way of Alaska, coming on foot from Asia across the land bridge that then joined Asia and North America. That happened during one of the earth's ice ages, when so much of the world's supply of water had frozen into ice caps and glaciers that the sea level dropped much lower.

The shallow ocean bottom between Alaska and Siberia was exposed so that animals and people could walk or even live on it. The land was much more than a mere bridge, for it was a vast area of roughly one million square miles connecting the two continents. Today this ancient land bridge is covered by water, and the area is now called Beringea.

Archaeologists have found along the Alaskan shores many clues to and proofs of the long ago migrations. There were at least four, and probably more, ice ages, each lasting thousands of years, with warming periods in between. During the cold periods the dry land would appear, allowing the people and creatures, many of them now extinct, to move to the new continent. The animals came first, and the people, Stone Age hunters, followed them, taking years, maybe generations, in the slow eastward movement.

They didn't come in an orderly fashion, for these were nomadic people looking for food or escaping from enemies. When they reached the North American continent some drifted south and east, and finally all of North and South America were populated by their descendants. It has been estimated that it took about seven thousand years for human beings to reach the tip of South America from the bridge in Alaska.

Because the bridge was so wide and the periods of migration went on for so many millenniums, various kinds of people came. The ancestors of today's Athapascan Indians, whose many branches live in Alaska's interior, probably came first. Then the Eskimos came, with the Inupiat Eskimos settling in the far north around the Arctic Ocean and the Yupik Eskimos moving farther south along the Bering Sea. Some of the Yupiks settled in the high lands that are now islands in the water between Siberia and Alaska. (Some scholars believe that the people who now live on St. Lawrence Island may have come from Asia at a later date.) The Eskimos' relatives, the Aleuts, settled in the Aleutian Islands and along the Alaska Peninsula. They gave Alaska her name, from the Aleut word "Alyeska," meaning "the Great Land." Archaeologists have not unraveled all the mysteries of the movements, origins, and relationships of the ancient

Ice-age people flee the woolly mammoth. An old print.

cultures, especially small groups such as the Eyaks and the Koniags.

The last ice age and the last land bridge ended about ten thousand years ago. The Indians of Alaska's southeast, the Tlingits and the Haidas, appear to have arrived a little later than that. Some people believe that they may have come by boat and foot through the Aleutian chain of islands, which, as the map shows, is itself a sort of bridge from Asia. Some of the people who settled in the Aleutian Islands came island-hopping from Asia, but other Aleuts are believed to have come by the northern land bridge through Beringea and moved south. Whatever, the archaeologists have found a complex puzzle when they try to reconstruct the past in prehistoric Alaska.

The groups of people often fought each other. Their languages and many of their customs and ideas differed, but they had many things in common, too, principally hunger. Life was a continual struggle for food.

Ruins of ancient Eskimo dwelling

Punuk figures, *left,* walrus ivory, St. Lawrence Island, circa A.D. 1000, from the author's collection. *Right,* Athapascan necklace, beads and porcupine quills on moose hide, from the author's collection.

They all felt a close kinship with the animals, although they ate them. All the early people felt that hunting and eating the wild creatures brought responsibilities. They had ceremonies of apology to the creatures, similar to the customs found today in some parts of Asia. They believed the fruits of the earth should be shared, so the strong hunters would divide meat with the old, sick, fatherless, and feeble of their tribe or village.

America's first people made shelters from whatever was available. Animal skins and bones, rocks, and dirt were used where there was no wood. Some far-northern Eskimos used blocks of snow and ice for building material.

The groups had special traditional crafts that have survived to this day. The Eskimos in the north had no wood so they became bone carvers to express their artistic nature. They often made charms and decorated weapons to please the animals they had to kill in order to survive. They used the fur of polar bears and seals to make warm and handsome clothes.

The Athapascan Indians in the interior had numerous animal skins for fashioning clothing. For decoration they sometimes flattened out porcupine quills and colored them with plant dyes. These quills were then painstakingly woven into soft caribou hides in artistic patterns.

The Aleuts who had marshy land covered with sea grass became famous

Tiny totem pole, from the
author's collection

Tlingit Indian chiefs at a potlatch

basket makers. They had so many birds that they could make ornate clothes of bird feathers.

The Tlingits and the Haidas, the last of the early people to come to Alaska, lived in the rain forests and were famous for their wooden totem poles carved from tree trunks. These great figures showed their family history and beliefs or served as family crests. Sometimes the symbols were carved or painted on houses and utensils. The Chilkat tribe of the Tlingit Indians used cedar bark and wool to weave these designs into ceremonial clothing and blankets. Rich chiefs sometimes gave lavish parties, called "potlatches," where raising new totem poles and wearing fancy clothes were part of the excitement.

All the groups drew deeply and gratefully from nature's gifts for their needs of clothing, shelter, food, and art.

Above, Eskimo masks. *Below*, Eskimo face.

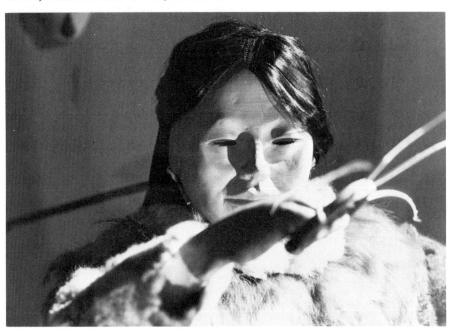

2 ❖❖❖

Some Ancient Poetic Beliefs

THE first Alaskans explained the wonders of nature and told their history by poetic myths. They healed their sick and asked the spirit world for special favors through certain wise people called shamans or *angakoks* or other terms in their own dialects. Most of the groups made masks and sang and acted out their traditional tales, often in a village "singing house."

Among the Yupik Eskimos the girls had a special kind of story-telling tool, the story knife. Fathers made these driftwood or walrus-tusk knives for their daughters so they could "draw" stories on the ice or smooth ground. Today Yupik girls still use story knives to show adventures of people and animals in a sort of comic-book style.

Over the thousands of years Alaska's Native people have had many tales to tell—tales of how the moon was a man and the sun his sister, and of magic trips to the moon by the village wise man who could leave his body and fly away. And then there was the story of Thunder and Lightning, the pair of abandoned twins who went to the sky to punish people who had been unkind to them.

The one creature who appears in all of Alaska's Native stories, whether Indian or Eskimo, is Raven, that mystic bird who has been forever lurking about the tents and houses, making fussy remarks in his croaking voice.

The Eskimos have a legend that Raven built Alaska; some of the Indians believed that Raven brought light and controlled the universe. Here is one of the stories the early people told long ago before any White people came to Alaska.

Raven Builds Alaska, An Eskimo Fable

The first creature of all was the magic Raven. One day Raven looked at his sooty black feathers, and he felt ugly and alone. Not far away he saw a graceful white swan. How I wish I had her for my wife, he thought.

So Raven wooed Swan in his croaking voice, and before long Swan agreed to marry him. They had a happy summer in the North, but then a problem arose.

"Raven," said Swan, "you know we didn't talk about this before our marriage, but I fly South with my fellow swans in the winter. You must come with us."

"But I stay North," argued Raven. "I must remain here to look

Raven builds Alaska, from the author's collection.

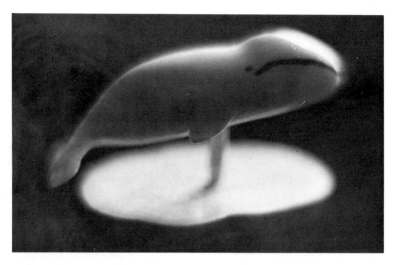

A little whale, Eskimo walrus ivory carving

after my kingdom. Stay with me. I will keep you warm."

But Swan would not agree to this, so Raven gave in and declared he would fly with the swans. Oh, how clumsy he was! In spite of trying with every muscle in his body, he could not make his wings fly far or fast. Soon he was falling behind, flapping helplessly as the swans swept gracefully forward.

"I will help you," said Swan, who loved Raven. "Get on my back."

But that didn't work, for Swan was soon tired of her heavy load. Even the other swans who tried to help had to give up.

"I can go no further," cried Raven in despair. Spying a rock far below in the salt water, he made up his mind to light there.

"Good-bye," he said to his wife and her relatives. "I will be here when you return in the spring."

"Good-bye, good-bye, Raven," called the swans as they waved their wings in farewell. "We know you will always be in the North."

So Raven plummeted to the spot in the sea below, flapping his wings just in time to land safely on the small rock. And there he sat, wet, cold, lonely, and miserable.

But good things always came Raven's way just when his misery was too great to bear. A baby whale flipped in the water!

"Hello," croaked Raven, and he reached over and pulled the little whale up onto the rock. Although Raven couldn't fly very easily, he

Eskimo walrus ivory carvings

was strong, and generous, and sociable, too, so he was glad to squeeze the little whale onto the rock beside him.

Raven was delighted with his new companion. He fussed and flapped over him, cawing a lullaby and amusing the baby whale with clumsy feats of flying. Just as the newborn whale began to respond to his new friend, the mother whale rose menacingly from the sea.

"Give me back my baby," she ordered.

"No," said Raven, "I am going to keep him here."

"Indeed you are not," spouted the mother whale. "I can make waves that will wash you and my baby right off that rock."

Raven knew this was true, for she was a very large whale. A crafty thought crept into his mind.

"If you will go down to the bottom of the sea and bring me some big rocks I will give you back your baby," he said.

The whale agreed and brought up some big rocks from the bottom of the sea.

"That's not enough," said Raven, pulling the baby closer to him. "I need more than that."

The whale brought more and more rocks. Finally Raven decided that he had enough. "But bring me some mud and gravel, so I can fill in the cracks," he said, looking at his rocky island. "Then you may have your baby."

So the whale brought up the mud and gravel, and Raven knew he had asked for enough.

"Very well, here is your baby," said Raven. And with great effort he pushed the little whale back into the sea to his mother.

Now alone, Raven amused himself by taking seaweed and mud and arranging them most beautifully around the rocks. Soon lichens and moss began to grow, and a few willows appeared. Raven was very proud of his new land. He planted little seeds that he caught from the wind, and they grew into big trees along the southeast coast.

Of course, such a beautiful land eventually attracted people and animals, but since Raven had built it from nothing but a rock sticking up from the sea, he always thought it was his land. To this day he considers himself the king of Alaska, and swans return every year as his loyal subjects.

3 ❖❖❖

Russians "Discover" Alaska

THE Eskimos and Indians of Alaska lived along in their harsh and hungry, and often happy, world for thousands of years, not dreaming that someday an outside force would bring great changes in their lives.

Nothing stays the same forever. Restless people dream of new ideas and look for new places to live. About the time the Pilgrims sailed from England to Massachusetts in the early 1600's, adventurous Russians were moving east into the wild land of Siberia.

The pioneering Russians who began to explore the land and trade furs with the native Siberians became known as Cossacks, from the Russian word *kazak*, meaning "adventurer." For many years the Cossacks kept pushing eastward to the sea, gradually covering the six thousand or so miles from the civilized capital city of St. Petersburg, which is now known as Leningrad.

Like the French and English and Spanish explorers who pushed westward across North America, the Cossacks built forts and villages, made trails and trading posts and crude maps, and fought the native tribes (who were doubtless relatives of the ancient people who had crossed over the land bridge thousands of years before). By the 1700's, some of the Russian frontiersmen had reached the Pacific, which they called the Eastern Ocean. Of course, the brave and the curious wondered what, if any, land lay across the uncharted water.

24

Eskimo dolls made of caribou horns in authentic dress, Kotzebue

Scholars and map makers knew a little about North America; the native people in Siberia who ran dog teams over the narrow strait in winter knew firsthand that there was inhabited land there. But the uneducated Cossacks did not know about these things. One might simply fall off the edge of the world, they reasoned, although some argued that the world was round.

Finally in the year 1658, Semeon Dezhnev, an energetic Cossack cursed with an itching foot and a restless imagination, said, "I'm going to see what's out there. . . ."

Dezhnev joined in one last wild fling of Cossack dancing and vodka drinking at a Siberian outpost and gathered some companions to go with him. In crude open boats they went on a voyage of exploration north on the Kolyma River and into the Arctic Ocean. They rounded the cape of land that stretched to the east and returned to Siberia by way of the Anadyr River.

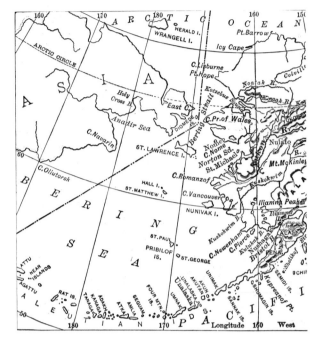

Old map shows East Cape, now Cape Dezhnev, around which Semeon Dezhnev sailed in 1658 to return home by the Anadyr River.

Old print of a Siberian hut

SIBERIAN HUT

Later he dictated an account of his voyage, but the paper was filed in a bureaucrat's cabinet in Siberia, only to be discovered many years later. A translation of Dezhnev's report says: "We were cold and hungry, naked and barefooted, and I poor Semeon and my companions went to the Anadyr in exactly ten weeks, reaching the stream low down near the sea."

The only honor Semeon got, and probably all he wanted, was the excitement of satisfying his curiosity about the land to the east.

4 ❖❖❖

Another Discovery of America, Vitus Bering's First Voyage

WHILE Semeon Dezhnev's report lay unread and nibbled by mice, Czar Peter the Great of Russia was putting forth all his energy to find out more about his great territory of Siberia and the mysterious land that lay across the sea to the east of it.

Although Czar Peter was rich and powerful and educated, he shared some of the qualities of his Cossack subjects: he was curious, and he liked to take chances. In the 1700's he summoned map makers, geographers, naturalists, astronomers, and historians to his court, bringing together scientists and scholars from all over Europe.

Peter and his educated advisors knew that the continent of North America lay east of Asia and west of Europe, and they knew about the voyages of Columbus and Magellan and other explorers. Peter sent expeditions to Siberia and Kamchatka, a peninsula that hangs like a beaver's tail from Siberia.

"Are Asia and the American continent connected by land?" pondered the great Czar. All the explorers and scholars could not answer that question. Learned men had brought him rare maps that showed legendary lands, but nobody knew much that could be counted on.

Peter had been enchanted with the sea since the day he became czar when he was only ten years of age.

A Russian church, old print

"I shall build a great navy for Russia," he vowed to himself when he was old enough to rule his vast country. "I want to find out if there is a Northeast Passage from Asia to America. I must find the most capable navigator to be had."

Since Russia had not had much of a navy in the past, Peter built it up by hiring good seamen from other countries to run the new Russian ships he had commissioned. One of these men was Vitus Bering, a Dane who had made voyages to the East Indies and served with a good record in the Russian Navy for over twenty years.

In 1724 Czar Peter appointed Captain Bering to command the expedition, for the glory of Russia, to find out if the continent of Asia was joined to North America. Bering was to build a ship on the Pacific

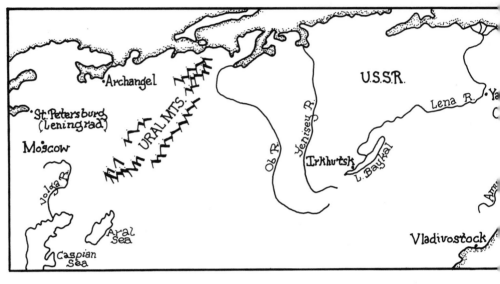

This map gives an idea of the vast distances the early Russian explorers took years to cross.

coast of Siberia, and to do it he would have to haul the materials over the six thousand miles or so from St. Petersburg. He set out in February, 1725, with thirty-three men and seventy-five wagonloads of supplies. The overland journey took more than two years, and the shipbuilding took another year, so that it was July 14, 1728, before Vitus Bering and his crew sailed from Kamchatka in the ship *St. Gabriel* to "discover America."

Czar Peter had died on the eve of Bering's departure from St. Petersburg, but Bering made the old czar's dream come true. After sailing north to about seventy miles above the Arctic Circle, Bering noted, on August 15, 1728, that they had passed between two points of land and entered an open sea. He decided that he had carried out his orders for he had determined that Asia and North America were separated by water. The water that divides Alaska and Siberia is today called the Bering Strait in honor of this man who made the official discovery for Russia.

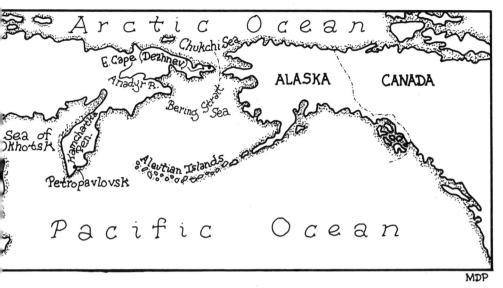

MDP

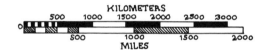

When Vitus Bering got back to St. Petersburg after carrying out his dangerous mission, some people criticized him for not going ashore to explore the new continent. This had not been part of his orders, but he volunteered to go again and investigate North America's west coast. So Empress Anna, the new Russian ruler, authorized the most expensive and complex expedition the world had ever seen.

She ordered naturalists, artists, agricultural experts, and astronomers to go along and help with the exploration. Specifically, they were to make maps and find out what riches and people lay in the mysterious new continent and if the legendary places on some of the maps actually existed. Captain Bering, the man in command, even had to build the ships to carry all these people and their equipment.

One could almost shed tears of sympathy for kindly Captain Bering, who, at fifty-two years of age, was considered an old man. The Empress

31

and all her advisors had put him in charge of a crew of temperamental people. There was a brash and brilliant young German naturalist Georg Stellar, who offended some people by wearing rough, smelly, skin clothes. He contradicted and bossed everyone in sight, and the fact that he was often right did not make him more popular. There was the noted French astronomer Louis Delisle de la Croyere, who dressed in satin waistcoats with lace cuffs and despised Stellar with all his heart. He constantly sniffed perfume to overcome the stench of Stellar's clothes. In contrast to Stellar's single knapsack, the astronomer took boxes and boxes of clocks and instruments, as well as a man to keep his equipment in order.

Moving the food, the scientific equipment, the baggage, the material for building the ships, and the people themselves on the trip from St. Petersburg to Kamchatka was incredibly difficult.

Captain Bering brought his wife along on the overland journey to the Pacific shore, and Lieutenant Sven Waxel, a young Swedish officer serving in the Russian Navy, brought his wife and family, too.

By the time the two ships were built and loaded to sail to America in the late spring of 1741, there was an unusual passenger on Captain Vitus Bering's ship. He was only a footnote in the official history of the voyage. Lieutenant Waxel's ten-year-old son Laurentz, who had somehow gained permission to go along on Russia's greatest voyage to explore America, was on board.

5 ❖❖❖

The Boy Who Went with Bering,
A True Adventure of Russian Alaska

Laurentz Waxel was a real boy who accompanied Captain Vitus Bering
on his renowned second voyage from Russia to North America in 1741.
From the log of the *St. Peter* and the journals of naturalist Georg
Stellar and of Laurentz' father, Lieutenant Sven Waxel, and other rare
documents concerning this expedition, Laurentz' story is reconstructed
in this could-be journal.

I, LAURENTZ Waxel, was a baby of only three years when our
family left St. Petersburg in the year 1733. Perhaps I remember this only
because my mother often told me the tale of the enormous preparations
for the great expedition and of her fears for taking me through the
frontier lands of Siberia. My father, Sven Waxel, who came from Sweden,
was then a lieutenant in the Imperial Russian Navy, and he had gained
permission to take his family along to Siberia.

I do vaguely recall snuggling under fur robes in the sleigh between my
mother and Madame Bering, and the warmth of the tea from the samovar
when we stopped at an inn or a house to sleep, before we reached that
part of Siberia where there were no inns and we set up tents for shelter.
It was April when we left our home with five hundred in our party. Oh,

Eighteenth-century house in Irkutsk, Siberia

how excited I was over the wagonloads of people, including sailors, soldiers, and shipbuilders, and the casks and cases of food and supplies! Other vans had gone ahead with material to build and outfit the ships.

When we reached Yakutsk in Siberia I was no longer a baby. I was still young in years but I was a veteran at riding rafts and open boats on rivers and in holding fast in dog teams or joggling in wagon seats, or even walking on my own sturdy feet. I was nearly seven years old when we left Yakutsk to head to Okhotsk, the outpost town that lies on the sea of the same name.

There the pressure of building the ships the *St. Peter* and the *St. Paul* kept everyone in an uproar. I remember how Captain Bering, who was always kind to me, grew aged with weariness as new problems arose. He and my father often talked of how impossible it was to carry out official orders from St. Petersburg. The people in the capital city did not seem to understand that there were no civilized supplies or helpers in this far-off land.

34

By the time the ships were nearing completion I was ten years old. I know I must have caused my mother many heartaches when I slipped out of the wretched hut, where we were housed, to climb the rigging, ask questions of the shipfitters, and get the smell of tar in my nostrils. This was a welcome relief after our house's stench of dried fish and reindeer, which was our daily fare.

When my mother would scold me, my father would take my side, saying, "Why, the lad's a born seaman. Even the great Czar Peter climbed the rigging of ships when he was no older than Laurentz."

My heart was heavy for I knew my father would soon be gone, maybe forever, certainly for a long time, and I would be left behind in Okhotsk with my mother and my two small brothers. Oh, how I wanted to go along when I listened to my father and Captain Bering talking of the details of the trip!

Captain Bering was to sail aboard the *St. Peter*, of which my father was second in command. Captain Alexei Chirikov would be in charge of the sister ship, the *St. Paul*, but both ships would be under the overall command of Captain Bering. The two ships were to stay together for protection, each ship with seventy-six persons aboard. I knew the vessels full well. They measured eighty by twenty by nine feet, were brigantine rigged, two masted, and bore fourteen cannon, for who knew what enemy might await them? Every nation in Europe was interested in the mysterious Pacific Ocean.

At times I felt we had enemies within our group, for there was constant quarreling between the scientists and the ships' officers. Indeed, even the officers were often at odds with each other, and it was hinted that Captain Chirikov openly showed disrespect for Captain Bering.

After some time in Okhotsk, my father arranged for our family to be moved to the new seaport of Avacha Bay on Kamchatka Peninsula on the Pacific Ocean. Captain Bering had a church built there where the hundreds of people who came to work on the final staging of the expedition could pray for the safety and success of the hazardous trip to America. I proved to be a good sailor on the vessel that carried us from Okhotsk to

Avacha, and in my head I was forming a great plan for myself.

Plans. . . . I shall return to my own plan, but I must tell about Captain Bering's plan that nearly went awry through no fault of his own, a mistake that nearly cost us the voyage. Whilst at the town of Yakutsk, Captain Bering had seen to the baking of a mountain of sea biscuit, enough to last the two ships for two years. He had planned to set sail early in the summer of 1741, to winter over in the mysterious America for exploring, and to return to Avacha the following summer in 1742. To do this, the ships must have enough food, for there was no assurance that there was food to be found in America.

So the precious biscuits were carried for hundreds of miles to Okhotsk where Captain Bering had them put aboard a smaller vessel to be shipped to Avacha, where the *St. Peter* and the *St. Paul* were to be loaded for the great expedition.

Sofron Khitrov, who commanded the ship carrying the biscuit, made a wretched blunder. He ran the ship aground on a sandbar, splitting open her side. Sea water rushed in over the biscuit, and the two years' supply of hard bread was lost forever. The expedition would have to resupply with what could be found locally, and that was not nearly enough for the long voyage.

My father and Captain Bering were not men given to swearing but, when news reached them that the foodstuff for the next two years was ruined, they swore. My mother and Madame Bering wept, and then we all went to church and prayed to a merciful God to help solve the problem.

According to the custom in the Russian Navy, each person on a vessel, however lowly his rank, could have a say in matters of grave concern to the ship. So all the people on the ships were consulted, and a plan was decided upon. They would sail as early as possible in the spring and return as late as possible that summer, making a shorter voyage due to the lack of food. This displeased the scientists, but it was the will of the majority not to run the risk of starvation.

36

Yet, from Khitrov's blunder I gained something for my own purposes as I will recount. While I had climbed around the *St. Peter* and the *St. Paul*, I had entertained the idea that I, Laurentz, should take this voyage to America along with my father. When I asked, my mother had said flatly "No," and when I whispered it to Captain Bering he had only laughed and tweaked my ear and said that I should wait a while, that the sea was eternal and would be there for me to conquer when I was man enough. My father replied that two years was too long for a boy to be away from home. All in all I had little hope, but when the ships' companies decided on a shorter trip I pleaded my case again.

"Father," I said, "I know about ships and travel."

"That you do," said my father.

"I proved a good sailor when we came from Okhotsk to Avacha," I went on.

"I must agree," said my father.

"Now the trip is made shorter. Please let me go too, *Dada*. I'll sleep on the deck and eat little. I can work as a midshipman."

"You are too young," said my father firmly. "You are only ten years old."

"But, Father, that is something I will overcome. Every day I grow older, don't I?"

This made my father laugh, and there was not much laughter these days. He promised to ask Captain Bering if I could go, and the captain agreed. In that way I became the first boy ever to sail across the Pacific Ocean on a Russian ship bound for America. I said my prayers and promised to do my best, and I hardly felt a tug at my heart to leave my mother and brothers. As my father recorded in his report of the voyage:

With God's help and a favorable wind we set sail from Avacha on June 4, 1741. The *St. Paul* came out of the bay ahead of the *St. Peter*, on which I was, and there outside she waited for us to catch her up, and when we had done so we set course together in the direction decided at the council.

And so I was at last at sea. Our officers were led astray by a foolish search. Had we sailed directly east, as it was computed later, we would have reached America in eight days, but alas, the orders from St. Petersburg were to follow a map in which my father and Captain Bering had no faith. We were instructed by Imperial Orders to search for Gama Land, a supposed island lying to the south between Asia and America. Few people believed it even existed, so the scientists in our party grumbled at the delay this would cause.

People are generally familiar with the main events of this voyage but I shall express my own feelings about some of those on the expedition, for, after all, I am the one who knows the things a lad observes at sea, things that are seldom put into a ship's log.

Gama Land did not exist, as we eventually found out, but in the vain search Captain Chirikov of the *St. Paul* lost us on the *St. Peter* in spite of the signals that had been arranged so that such a mishap would not occur. Many said that Captain Chirikov did it by intention, for he did not like being under the orders of Captain Bering. At any rate we searched many days for the *St. Paul*, losing valuable time.

Finally Captain Bering abandoned the search and we headed north into uncharted waters. Once we sighted a whale, thinking it was land, but we took it as a good omen, and on July 16 the naturalist Stellar said he knew positively that land lay ahead.

Perhaps this is the place to write a few lines about this unusual man who was so hated by the crew. I confess I had a liking for him, and so did Captain Bering, most of the time. Mr. Stellar was young and full of energy and ideas, a physician and a naturalist. He did not hold with carrying much baggage as did our other scientists. He merely slung a knapsack across his back, and for clothes he preferred to dress as the native people did in animal hides.

When I asked outright why his jacket smelled so dreadful he answered that it had been cured by soaking it in urine and ashes and made soft by rubbing it with reindeer brains and tallow. I thought he was joking,

Carving of seal, walrus ivory, modern, St. Lawrence Island

but after living in close quarters with him I soon believed that it was true. Well educated in the universities of Europe but made sour because his wife had left him, Stellar took pleasure in parading his superior knowledge before the rest of the ship's company until most of the sailors would have gladly seen him burn in the inferno. But he knew more about the natural world than any man I ever met.

So when Mr. Stellar announced he sensed land because of the change in the sea vegetation, he only met with jeers from the less learned. But he was right. The next day ahead of us loomed great snow-covered mountains which Captain Bering named for St. Elias, on whose day our good fortune occurred. It was noted in the log of the *St. Peter* on July 17, 1741.

When within a few days we were able to maneuver the ship so we could land on an offshore island, Mr. Stellar was wild with eagerness to go ashore to explore and collect specimens of birds and plants and animals. He was eager to locate and observe native people if such were there. Also, Mr. Stellar had driven the crew half insane telling them over and over of his theories of how to cure the scurvy. He said men on ships should eat

Carving of whale, walrus ivory, modern

green plants from sea and shore and in that way scurvy would not overtake them—an idea he repeated until some scoffed at him or even cursed him, for it seemed foolish at the time.

Perhaps to punish Mr. Stellar for his irritating habits, Captain Bering would not at first allow him to go ashore but instead put Khitrov, that same one who ruined the biscuits and thus changed the course of our trip, in charge of a small boat to fetch water for the ship. I confess Mr. Stellar behaved most abominably, speaking with rude vexation to the Captain in the presence of the crew. Captain Bering did finally allow Mr. Stellar to go ashore. I wanted much to go, too, but I was not permitted.

However, Mr. Stellar, who loved an audience, told me all about his adventures as the first naturalist to visit the Pacific shores of North America, for so he considered himself. Although he had only ten hours ashore, he found bountiful sea otters, and black and red foxes so tame that they followed at his heels, and ravens and magpies eating among the kelp.

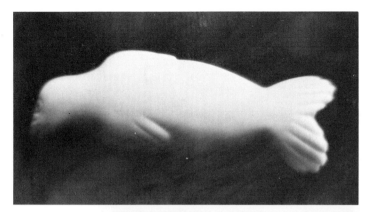

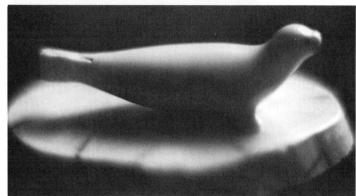

Eskimo walrus
ivory carvings,
typical motifs

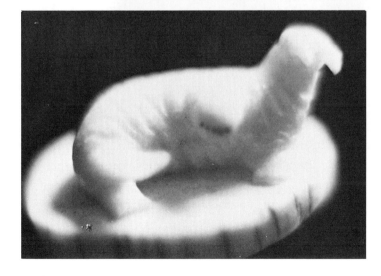

Mr. Stellar found a hollowed-out log filled with water where American Natives had been cooking. They had dropped stones into the water to heat it to boil food. He found what he thought were reindeer bones and sheep bones, as well as dried fish ready for eating. He found trees cut with stone or bone axes.

There were giant spruce trees with thick moss. He even found a house of sorts, a tree-covered cellar hole which made him think that Americans live underground. But he saw no people, only their baskets and arrows and utensils and nets made of seaweed. He saw smoke, proving that people were not far away, probably hiding. He identified cranberries and salmonberries, and he shot and brought back a bright-colored bird, which we named Stellar's jay.

Stellar had taken some items from the Americans' dwelling and thought that some gift should be left in their place to prove friendship. So Captain Bering ordered the boatswain to leave an iron kettle and some trinkets to replace the things our Russians had taken. Stellar's heart was about to break when Captain Bering ordered the ship to set sail back to Avacha the next morning, with no further chance to explore or to meet the Natives.

My father, too, was disappointed and astonished, but he understood that Captain Bering was a sick man, beginning to show signs of the scurvy. He knew that the Captain did indeed have the responsibility to get the *St. Peter* and her crew back to Avacha by mid-September as agreed in the beginning. Accordingly, we set our sails back to Siberia as we rolled in the unknown ocean.

Rough days at sea followed. My father was bent with responsibility because Captain Bering was almost too ill to leave his cabin or make decisions. Constant headwinds, terrible fogs, shoals, and rocks, along with the lack of charts, made life a constant hazard. I fancy that my father was sorry he had brought me for he feared we would all perish. He kept me close to his side, and Stellar kept me dosed with his fresh herbs, some of which I pressed upon my father. To this day I thank the man Stellar, for his strange medication kept my father and me free of the scurvy that was beginning to spread on the ship.

On August 1 we sighted land, and for days we skirted islands but did not go ashore. Stellar observed a strange, whiskered animal about five feet long with a head like a dog's. It was a gray and reddish color and it had fins on its tail. He called me to his side to see. He told me it was a sea monkey, but we never saw another, nor did anybody else in the world as far as I know.

Three weeks had gone by since we left St. Elias, and September was almost upon us. Drinking water was again becoming low. On August 28 there were new signs of land, and on the next day we found a safe anchorage. The sailor Nikita Shumagin, who had been kind to me, died of scurvy before we anchored, and we buried him on the land which we named Shumagin Island in his honor.

Mr. Stellar was allowed at last to go with the water detail. The men, resenting Stellar, refused to carry the fresh water he located, instead bringing partly salty water, which later caused grave problems on the

Aleuts in bidarkas

Eskimo hunter, soapstone

ship. He found many new birds and fish, but this did not help his anger when he found that crafty Khitrov had gone ashore himself to communicate with the Natives, mostly to annoy Stellar who so yearned to make such a study. It was a small satisfaction that Khitrov came to grief. He lost the ship's small yawl and very nearly lost the lives of those in his care during this little exploit, but we rescued all the men, although the boat was lost.

Then luck changed for Stellar, and me, too. On September 5, as the *St. Peter* was anchored near an island, we heard human voices. Soon two small sealskin boats with one man in each came out from the shore. We called to them, and waved in a friendly manner, but they could not understand the Chukchi interpreter we had brought from Siberia, hoping that American Natives might recognize his tongue.

So my father got into our long boat, squeezing me between himself and Mr. Stellar, and we rowed toward the shore with gifts for the Americans. These they would not accept, but instead they seized our interpreter. Father gave the order to fire two guns in the air. On this the Americans let the interpreter go free, and we cut our anchor and returned in haste to the *St. Peter*.

I saw the Americans at close range, and they looked like our Chukchi interpreter, except that they had made holes in their faces and had stuck bones and sticks in their noses for ornaments. The next day nine more Americans paddled toward our ship, but they would not come abroad. Although they had metal knives, we believed they had never seen firearms before.

Battling headwinds again, we set out for weeks of roaring seas and autumn gales. More men were dying with scurvy, and Captain Bering was very ill. My father was now in total command of the ship. So many were sick that the few who were well had a desperate time doing the work, and I took on a man's responsibilities as much as I was able. Burials at sea were almost a daily affair. My father himself began to show signs of scurvy so that he could scarcely move about. Our water was nearly gone, and I tried to cheer my father, remembering that I had promised to serve him well when he agreed to let me come on this trip.

On November 7 we landed on an island, and my father, very weak, took me with him when he went ashore to find water and look for a suitable place to land the sick, for we who had survived to this point decided that we could sail no further. Twelve of our company were dead and thirty-four were totally disabled.

On November 10 we began to take the sick from the ship to the cold shore of this unfriendly windswept island. There were no Natives to aid us or resist us, and no longer did the men quarrel with Stellar, whose good health and good sense were literal lifesavers now.

We made shelters by digging holes in the ground and covering them with sails. I, Laurentz, was no longer treated as a lad because I did man's work. By early December the *St. Peter* was vacated, and a strong wind blew it up onto the shore. We were wretched with the snow, hail, rain, and continual darkness. There were no bushes or trees for shelter, and we had only creeping willow and driftwood for fires. A small amount of rye flour was all that was left for food.

On December 8, 1741, Captain Bering died and we buried him with honors and named the island in his memory. Bering Island, I know now, lies at 55°N. and 166°E., but then we did not know exactly where we were.

Now my father was totally in command. Food was the main problem. We who were able had to forage for those who were too sick to hunt. Mr. Stellar and I and a few other healthy ones captured some sea otters, a tough but welcome dish to eat, and much prized for their furs. Stellar showed us roots to dig and eat, and our health improved. Our spirits rose a little when Father told the men they could play cards, a sport usually forbidden in the Russian Navy, for he felt that it would help while away the dark cold hours, especially for the feeble.

Luck changed when a dead whale washed ashore. Its blubber made us warm, and it was more pleasant to eat than sea otter, which had to be chewed and chewed and downed bit by bit, extending its repulsive taste.

We stirred our ration of rye with warm water and let it stand until sour and then fried it, washing it down with tea made of roots. My father shared his rations with me, for I was now almost twelve years old and had a healthy appetite. I wanted as much to eat as my father, but we reached an agreement that he who had three spoons of bread at morning would have two in the evening, and he who had two in the morning would have three at night.

Soon we learned to capture and eat sea lions and seals, great delicacies both. Mr. Stellar was indeed happy, for he roamed the island exploring. He made himself a waterproof coat of seal intestines so that, rain or fair,

Sea cow and sea lions, drawn by Stellar

he was out sketching and listing the flowers, mosses, birds, and sea animals. Especially did he observe the sea cow, such a wonderfully edible animal that it cheered us all.

Watching Mr. Stellar make his notes in careful Latin caused me to learn some methods of natural observation. He believed that these strange sea cows, which measured over thirty feet in length and about twenty-five in girth and weighed about eight thousand pounds by his estimate, were related to land animals ancestral to the elephant, for their upper part resembled a land animal whilst the tail was that of a fish. They masticated their food like cows. Mr. Stellar carefully mounted a specimen and filled it with dried grass so that it could be displayed in a museum in Russia.

Stellar makes the first measurement of a sea cow, Bering Island, July 12, 1742. Drawn by Stellar, reconstructed by L. Stejneger.

Stellar was at last appreciated. My father wrote in his log, "From my own experience I can assert that none of us became well before we began eating something green, plant or root." By following Stellar's advice our health improved steadily, and the coming of spring with the mating of the foxes and the nesting of the birds, put joy in our hearts with the hope of returning home.

We had decided that when April came we would break up the remains of the *St. Peter* and make a new ship with the salvaged materials. When we laid the keel of the new vessel on May 5, my father celebrated by serving all hands a drink of tea soup, which for lack of better ingredients was made with musty rye flour and fish oil.

Of the seventy-six men who had left Avacha in June, 1741, thirty-one were dead. The forty-five of us who had survived worked with a strong will to make the new ship, but it was August 13 before we could set sail in the second *St. Peter*, as she was christened.

As the ship was too small for ought but our bodies, my father was forced to order people to leave behind many belongings, such as valuable skins that would have meant money on our return. Stellar's heart was broken that he could not take along his preserved sea cow, but as my father pointed out, if the enormous specimen went, then human beings would have to stay behind. When it was discovered at the end of the voyage that wily Khitrov had secreted sea otter skins which he sold for a great price, my anger knew no bounds.

When we landed at Avacha on August 27, 1742, we found we had been given up for dead. Great was the rejoicing, especially by my mother, but there was sorrow for the death of our great Captain Bering. We gathered at the Church of St. Peter and St. Paul and had a service of thanksgiving to Almighty God for our preservation, and we fulfilled our dying commander's request by making an ikon of St. Peter in a casing of silver.

Our sister ship *St. Paul* had been brought back by Captain Chirikov the previous autumn. He had landed men on the American shore too, a few days prior to our shore party from the *St. Peter* it was claimed, but with a grim disaster. When the men who went ashore failed to return, Captain Chirikov sent his only other small boat to search for them, and it also disappeared, a loss of fifteen men. As none lived to tell the tale, who knows what they saw? Perhaps they are living there today among the Americans; their fate has not been discovered, to my knowledge. The *St. Paul* had returned to Avacha in October, 1741, with most of the remaining men dying of scurvy. With no small boat to take men ashore, they had had no way to get fresh water, adding more misery to their journey.

Now in this year of 1750, I, Laurentz Waxel, am nearing twenty and will soon become an officer in the Russian Navy. Mr. Stellar died on the return trip to St. Petersburg, still a young man, and sadly lamented by those of us who had become his friends. None of the training I have received to become a naval officer was as rigorous as the experiences I had as the first Russian boy to make a voyage of exploration to America.

Laurentz Waxel became a distinguished naval officer. In 1778 Laurentz Waxel, then forty-eight years old, and his two brothers were made Russian noblemen by Empress Catherine the Great. In 1778 the American Revolution was at its height; Baron Laurentz Waxel and General George Washington were about the same age.

6 ❖❖❖

The Russians Arrive:
A Woman, Furs, and a Colony

THE deceitful scheme of Sofron Khitrov to fool the others by bringing otter pelts back to Russia had a far-reaching effect. The eyes of greedy merchants glistened when the news of a rich new hunting area got around. Now that it had been proved without a doubt that America was there, filled with otters for the taking, the fur rush began. Brave, but often insensitive, men set out in makeshift vessels, using the newly made maps. The idea of conserving wildlife did not occur to hunters who were lucky enough to survive the trip. The otter population began a downward course, and most of the traders treated the Native Americans so badly that it became a scandal reported to the Russian court, angering Her Majesty, Empress Catherine the Great.

One of the most memorable men to get rich in Alaska's fur trade was brash young Grigori Shelikhov, who was only twenty years old in 1767 when he showed up in the Siberian town of Irkutsk, eager to go to America. He went on a voyage or two, and soon this ambitious young man was ready for a unique venture. He had a shrewd wife, Natalia; a partner with financial backing; three ships with supplies; and nearly two hundred followers organized at Okhotsk. He was going to found the first Russian colony in America to be a center for fur trading.

In 1783, Shelikhov and his intrepid Natalia, who would be the first

white woman in Russian America, as the area was being called by then, boarded ship for America, leaving their three children behind with relatives. Shocking! But the Shelikhovs were shocking people: Grigori did not even have a beard, an unheard of thing for an ordinary Russian man.

They had troubles aplenty en route—shipwreck, near starvation, hostile Natives, among other disasters. It was a year later that they finally disembarked at Kodiak Island to begin America's first Russian settlement, which they named Three Saints. Shelikhov and his helpers built a tiny village of about a dozen huts, and a few outposts, and got along well enough with the people on Kodiak Island, who are known as Koniags and are related to Eskimos and Aleuts. A few fur traders who had come earlier and tried to take over the island had not succeeded, but Grigori Shelikhov and his wife managed to bring the area under Russian control. Sturdy and brave, Natalia, with her white skin and European clothes, was a source of wonder to the Natives.

After four years the Shelikhovs left the infant colony in the hands of a fellow Russian and returned home, reaching Irkutsk in 1787 with many bundles of furs. They found their children were thriving and had grown amazingly during their parents' journey to America.

Shelikhov had a grand dream of quickly setting up a Russian empire in the new world, but he needed money and authority and the support of his empress, Catherine. He wanted a monopoly of the fur trade for Russia—and for himself. To get the attention of the unpredictable empress, he told a lot of outright lies about his American settlement, saying that he had built a church and schools and that they needed serfs, as the Russian peasant slaves were called, to work on the great farms he had laid out.

He even said that the Native Americans were crying out for mission-

Aleuts in bidarkas, Russian representation

aries to teach them Christianity, which was hardly the case, since the Indians, Aleuts, and Eskimos had their own ancient ideas of religion. He tried every trick he could dream up to soften the heart of Her Imperial Highness. Finally his luck changed. His company was granted certain special rights and, to the surprise, and discomfort, of the loose-tongued Shelikhov, the government also provided priests, missionaries, and serfs, a crowd of four hundred people in all, for the little settlement of Three Saints—where there was no church, no school, no cleared farmland, and no housing. Certainly there was no prospect of a warm welcome from the Native people of Kodiak, thought Shelikhov uneasily. The Natives generally fought and hated the invading Russians.

Part of Shelikhov's success with the empress was that the Shelikhovs' daughter had married an influential young nobleman, Nickolai Rezanov. It was he who convinced the ruler that Shelikhov was getting along well with the Americans. This appealed to Empress Catherine, for she apparently had been concerned about reports that Russian traders had abused the Aleuts and Indians and Eskimos.

The embarrassed Shelikhovs themselves decided not to return to America just yet, probably out of fear for their lives when the shiploads of people going to the colony found out how badly they had been deceived! The couple remained behind in Siberia where Shelikhov died in the summer of 1795 without ever returning to Three Saints. Natalia became head of her husband's company, and one of her first duties was to open and destroy the letters of rage that came from the new colony when the newcomers got there, expecting a splendid city and instead finding themselves marooned on what they considered a desert island. Certainly there was not enough food or supplies for them all, let alone housing.

In 1799 Natalia Shelikhov, who was a clever businesswoman, with the help of her son-in-law engineered a union of all the fur-trading companies in Russian America into one great body, the Russian American Company. It was a big organization with government backing, and Natalia was one of the chief stockholders.

Shelikhov's grave in Irkutsk

A rich widow, this first white woman to have lived in Russian America settled in St. Petersburg, where she and her children were made members of the nobility and lived in luxury and high style for the rest of their lives.

But one good thing Grigori Shelikhov had done five years before he died was to hire a manager for his colony. Alexander Baranov, the new manager, was to become the most famous of all Russian Americans.

7 ❖❖❖

The Amazing Alexander Baranov,
A Russian-American Folk Hero

ALEXANDER Baranov didn't want to go to America when Grigori Shelikhov asked him to leave Siberia in 1790 and travel to faraway Kodiak to manage the struggling colony there. He gave a flat "No" for an answer and stared moodily at the sea, cursing his recent run of bad luck. He had been robbed by Siberian Chukchi tribesmen of the furs he had gathered with painful hardship, and now he was faced with overwhelming debts.

"Don't you see, this will solve your problems?" begged Shelikhov. "If you'll agree to go to America for five years we'll pay you well." Shelikhov knew Baranov's reputation for being bright, brave, and honest. He was just the man for the post.

Baranov thought some more, recalling how his life had improved when he, an illiterate boy, had run away from his lowly home far away in western Russia to seek his fortune in Moscow. In the city he had not only learned to read and write Russian but German as well, so that he could read books on science. This knowledge had inspired his restless mind to bring him all the way across Siberia so he could learn more geography and natural science firsthand.

He liked the challenge of trying new things and going new places, but hearing of the scandalous behavior of the Russian traders in America, he wanted no part of it. His countrymen had claimed American territory

Unalaska, early print

since the days of Vitus Bering, exacting furs from the Natives as tribute for Russia's monarchs. He knew they had kidnapped women, turned men into slaves, stolen furs, and behaved as no good Russian should. He knew, too, that Shelikhov was a noted liar. Should he, Baranov, an honest man, get involved in this colonial scheme?

"Alexander," said his old friend, the district military commander in Okhotsk, Siberia, "do it. Go. North America needs enterprising good men like yourself. You must do it for Mother Russia if for no other reason."

And so it was that, half for patriotism, half to meet an inner challenge, Alexander Baranov watched the coast of Asia grow smaller in the distance as he stood on the deck of a worn-out ship with a drunken captain, bound for America.

In no time the passengers were pressed into manning the pumps as the leaky old vessel wallowed in heavy seas. For four weeks they battled headwinds, surviving on a cup of water a day for each person, along with meager rations. In October they reached Unalaska Island in the Aleutians, stopping to replenish their water. While at anchor a storm blew the ship onto some rocks, and all hope of reaching Kodiak that winter was lost as they abandoned the craft, working feverishly to save the cargo.

Baranov, taking charge as general manager of the Russian American Company now that they were on shore, set out to make friends with the Native Aleuts who lived in roofed-over holes dug in the sand. The Russians stared at the Aleuts, whose idea of beauty was to alter their mouths with pieces of bone stuck into their lower lips and to decorate their faces with tattoos and unusual markings. But the newcomers learned to appreciate the agreeable Aleuts.

"Dig holes in the sand, and make roofs with the sails of the ship so we can have a place to live," Baranov ordered the Russians. "Copy the houses of the Aleuts."

Baranov learned the Aleut language, and soon the Native people were helping the Russians, sharing with them their delicacy of cranberries in fish oil, as well as dried salmon, *yukola*, which the Russians found not to their taste. Some of the Russians died as the bitter winter storms battered them in the darkness, but those who survived followed the inspiration of Baranov and learned the Native ways. They dug for roots to stave off scurvy, they hunted sea otter, and they made rain clothes of seal gut and warm garments of bird feathers. When longer hours of light and a lessening of the winter winds told them that spring was coming, they made small open boats from the ship's wreckage. Persuading some of the Aleuts to go with them, they sailed to Kodiak, arriving at Shelikhov's settlement just about a year after they had left Okhotsk.

The general manager found the supplies low and the population increased, with dozens of new half-Russian children, called Creoles, born to Native mothers. Baranov himself was sick with fever, but he began at once to explore the area by foot and small boat, planning how he would extend the holdings of his company and plant copper shields bearing Russia's Imperial coat of arms to show that this was Russian territory. He also began gathering furs from the Indians, for that was the main purpose of the Russian colony.

Russian double eagle, copper marker to indicate Russian territory

Baranov had feared problems, but he never dreamed of the dreadful mess that he had to endure in his first few years in Russian America. The discontented serfs, the temperamental priests, and the disgruntled colonists that Shelikhov had sent finally arrived in 1792, and they nearly drove Baranov to suicide. The Natives fought the invading Russians constantly, although they were not a united force. Baranov soon found that the Indians on Kodiak Island hated and feared the Tlingit coastal Indians, and that the Indians and Eskimos were ancient enemies. All the Natives wanted firearms, and Baranov lived in dread of that. The Russians were forbidden to trade firearms to the Natives, but ships from other nations were exploring the North Pacific. These foreigners would not hesitate to provide guns to drive out the Russians.

Baranov yearned to be allowed to return to Russia, but there was no word from headquarters and no way to leave. So he learned to cope. He

Three studies of Eskimo faces: *above,* Natives of the Coast near Cape Thomson; *below,* "Three Men" by Kivetoruk Moses of Nome; *and opposite,*

Eskimo dolls

was tactful and friendly, sensible and strong, in his dealings with the Indians. He made friends with the Eskimos who lived across the Alaska Peninsula on Bristol Bay. When he admired their fur garments, he found they were eager to trade furs for iron and other European manufactured goods that the Russian ships should be bringing soon.

It was in this uneasy atmosphere that European industrial civilization reached Alaska, headed by this brave, troubled, diminutive man.

8 ❖❖❖

The Story of Alaska's First Shipbuilding

SINCE it was ships that brought men and supplies across the Pacific, sturdy vessels were essential to Russian America. Yet the officials in Russia seemed to care too little, or lacked money, or simply forgot to send the ships and supplies to their colony. Or, as it often happened, ships were wrecked en route.

When, in 1792, the first Russian supply ship since Baranov's arrival in the colony, the *Eagle,* sailed into Kodiak, it was hailed with riotous joy. Vodka! Tea! Mail!

When Baranov opened the letters from Shelikhov he found orders to build his own ship, along with the news that the necessary materials were on board the *Eagle,* which was commanded by an Englishman, James Shields, a man experienced in shipbuilding. Now the colony could have its own transportation. There were shouts and huzzahs and feasting on the food that had come in the cargo.

The shipbuilding project involved more of Shelikhov's lies and irresponsibility. He had sent no cloth for sails, no tools, little tar, and not enough copper and brass. Baranov swore and wept in classic Russian fashion. How could Shelikhov order him to build a ship without adequate material? Headquarters had not even sent enough naval stores to repair the supply ship!

Alexander Baranov

But Baranov was a stubborn man. Out of sheer determination and courage he decided to try. He'd show them! Surely somewhere, somehow, in this vast North America, there must be the things necessary to build a ship.

Captain Shields only laughed. "You can't build a ship here in this Godforsaken place with no civilized material," he said. But then he added, "Well, I must confess that there is splendid timber to be had on some of the coastal areas."

Baranov had read books on mineralogy, and he had been exploring the natural resources of the area. He knew there was coal, and even iron ore, nearby, although there was no simple way to get it into usable form. But he began gathering up all the old iron objects in the colony.

Every man, woman, and child was sent out on a giant metal hunt.

They dug in the sands and waters, looking for scrap iron from old shipwrecks. Native people were persuaded to sell or trade their bits of metal. Then Baranov began a charcoal industry to attempt to smelt his own iron, although it didn't work out very well. He set up a forge and began to make nails and bolts from the pile of collected scrap metal.

Captain Shields, who planned to return to Russia soon, watched the mad genius with amusement, especially when Baranov showed him his ambitious sketch of the ship he planned to build, a three-masted sailing vessel with two decks, seventy-nine feet long. Then Baranov took a deep breath and confronted Shields with authority in his voice.

"You're not going back to Russia this year, Captain Shields," said the manager. "You're going to stay here in Russian America and explore and collect otter skins while I turn my attention to building this ship. Then you are going to teach me to sail it."

The argument that followed was so violent that it ended in a fistfight on the split log floor. Finally, both bruised men rose and faced each other levelly.

"As local manager of the Russian American Company I have the authority to order you to stay," said Baranov. "Here it is, written in the Company rules."

Shields, a good loser, laughed and shook his head, rubbing the lump on his forehead. Baranov was the most stubborn man he had ever met, and Shields decided at that moment to do all he could to help him.

"So I will teach you to build ships and navigate, Alexander," he said. "Then you can be your own master when the ship is built, for with a will like yours I know it will be built."

Navigation! That was the greatest gift a man could bestow, for the secrets of navigation were carefully guarded by a tight group of experts in those days.

Baranov and the men chosen to help him moved the scrap iron to Resurrection Bay, near the present town of Seward. For tools they had only the same old axes, but there was plenty of timber nearby. For caulk-

Russian ikon

ing they tapped trees for pitch which they mixed with moss from the forest. Tar was contrived from spruce gum and oil, and a combination of whale oil and ochre produced a protective paint.

Food for the work force was a constant problem, and troubles arose at Kodiak where men stole commissary supplies the minute Baranov left the island. But Baranov kept on, driving his workers to exhaustion while keeping their spirits high with praise. He worked them until sweat froze on their hands, and they grumbled but kept working when there was nothing to eat but *yukola*, that dried salmon that the Russians found so repulsive, and there was no tea or vodka to cheer their spirits.

There was always trouble with the Indians, even friendly tribes, but the work on the ship kept going. Baranov was forced to take outlaw justice into his hands and imprison a Russian from a competing Russian company who had caused grave problems with the Native people. Only

God knew how the authorities in Russia would react when they heard about that!

And still the shipbuilding kept on, forced by this small man who was driven by a strange inner fire of his own. Was it patriotism, pride, or just brute determination to finish what he had begun that kept Baranov moving his ship to completion?

In August, 1794, the ship was launched. "I christen you *Phoenix*," said Baranov proudly, breaking a bottle of precious vodka on her bow as she slid down the ways.

When a few weeks later the *Phoenix* embarked on her maiden voyage from Resurrection Bay to Kodiak, her sails were made of scraps and rags and old tents, but to Alexander Baranov there was never so beautiful a sight.

The *Phoenix* sailed across the Pacific to Siberia the following summer, commanded by the great-hearted Shields, who had taught Baranov the secrets of navigation before he left. She made the trip in about a month, a record run across the northern Pacific in the year 1795.

Russian America had produced a miracle of sorts.

9 ❖❖❖

The Marriage of an Indian Princess

ONE of Alexander Baranov's joys was his marriage to an Indian princess. Here is how it came about.

When in 1792 an earthquake split apart a third of the buildings in the headquarters village of Three Saints, Baranov worked like a dynamo to build a new settlement in a safer spot nearby at St. Paul Harbor, also on Kodiak Island.

The Russians still had no tools except axes, but Baranov led the work by cutting down the first tree for the logs to build the new town. Driving the men like the archfiend that they often called him, he nevertheless got the town built and set out at once in a small boat with a few companions to explore the mainland. He had to make friends with the Indians to do this, an uncertain venture full of danger. He wanted to meet the Indians who lived at the upper end of Prince William Sound (near the present town of Valdez, where the Alyeska pipeline pumps oil into ships in modern times).

Baranov was well aware that the Indians might kill him, for European ships had visited Prince William Sound before, sometimes cheating, fighting, and abusing the Indians. There was no reason for the local people to trust the Russians, but Baranov intended to try to improve relations.

Interior of Tlingit house

Tlingit doll—perhaps Baranov's princess

The Natives lived in long communal buildings, sometimes fifty feet in length, and the families cooked over fires in the center, with the smoke going through holes in the roof. Baranov and his men were received, but not very cordially, into the chief's house, probably because the chief wanted to tell Baranov, through a translator, about all the wicked deeds done previously by Europeans to his people.

Baranov listened with sympathy and presented the chief with a copper imperial insignia of Russia, and told him that the great ruler in Russia would protect the Indians from foreign invaders in the future if the chief would agree to be his friend. Baranov was lucky; he didn't know that a flat piece of copper had tribal significance to the local people. The chief, very pleased, then gave Baranov a copper circle, and they formally became friends.

And then the chief clapped his hands and before them in the light of the fires appeared an Indian girl dressed entirely in white buckskin.

69

Tlingit dolls—perhaps the wedding

She was tall and straight with lustrous black hair falling to her waist. Her skin was smooth and her cheeks were pink, and she walked with pride, her eyes shyly cast down. She was the seventeen-year-old daughter of the chief himself.

"You may have her for a wife," said the old chief. "It will make our friendship last."

Baranov was dumbfounded. Realizing that she was no ordinary girl to be carried away lightly, he accepted her for a bride but said he would return for her with appropriate ceremony.

"She is too young now," said Baranov, and this pleased the Indians who thought highly of their princess.

It was two years, years filled with turmoil and fighting for Baranov, before he brought his Indian princess to Kodiak in 1794. He called her Anna Grigoryevna and treated her like the princess she was, providing her with servants. He draped a silk scarf over her head in the Russian manner and gave her golden earrings for a wedding present.

They were happy together for many years and had two children— a boy and a girl, Antipetr and Irina, who were brought up as Russians and educated by the priests in the Russian American schools which by then had been established in the colony. Baranov had a piano brought from Russia so Irina could learn music. A beauty like her mother, in time Irina married a young Russian naval officer who became Baranov's successor as manager of the Russian American Company. Antipetr attended the Imperial Cadet School in St. Petersburg. Eventually Irina and her husband went to St. Petersburg to live, and their mother, Princess Anna, returned to her own Indian people, living out her days on a pension provided by Baranov.

10 ❖❖❖

The End of the Baranov Era

WHEN in 1819 Baranov, honored, but old and ill, retired as manager of the Russian American Company, he prepared to return to Russia. He could look back on warfare and expansion, strife and affection, constant excitement and danger. There had been great events like the visit of nobleman Nikolai Rezanov, Shelikhov's son-in-law, who brought a fine library to the new settlement, Sitka. Rezanov was impressed by the manager's elegant house, "Baranov's Castle," which overlooked the town. He left full of praise for Baranov. And there had been the proud moment when Baranov's work was officially recognized and he was made a Collegiate Councilor in the Imperial Government, an honor that made him worthy of being addressed as "Excellency."

He was proud that Russian America now had twenty-four settlements, more or less, ranging from the arctic to California and far out into the Aleutian Islands. There were four hundred pure Russians and an equal number of part Russian people. There were schools for the children, and missionaries had firmly established the Russian Orthodox Church in North America (despite quite a few fights with Baranov who did not always agree with them).

And riches? Manager Baranov had made the Russian American Company wealthy and had kept the books honestly and dispensed justice the

Early view of Sitka (New Archangel)

best he could, although sometimes by ruthless means. He was seventy-two years old, and tears streamed down his face as he said good-bye to Russian America and his "Castle." He was on his way home to Mother Russia.

He never got there. He died in April, 1819, and was buried at sea. That is why people say today that Alexander Baranov's ghost comes in with the fog from the sea along the Alaskan coast where he gave thirty vital years of his life.

11 ❖❖❖

Some People and Things to Remember About Russian America, Including a Special Christmas Tree

No tales of Russian Alaska would be complete without mentioning Father Ivan Veniaminov, who came to the Aleutian Islands as a missionary priest of the Russian Orthodox Church in 1824. He opened schools, wrote down folk stories of the local people, made studies of their history, wrote dictionaries, and built churches. He was honest, tolerant, and brilliant. He left his mark not only on Alaska but on Russia, too, for in 1868, after a notable career in Alaska and Siberia, the Czar appointed him to the position of "Metropolitan of Moscow and Kolumna," which made him the head of the Russian Church. Alaska's beloved Father Veniaminov became known all over the world as Metropolitan Innocent.

Among the managers of the Russian American Company who followed Baranov was Baron Ferdinand Wrangell, an explorer with an inquiring mind, who left a mark on Alaska where he arrived with his bride in 1830. Wrangell had married a noblewoman, after a mere two weeks of romantic courtship, a beauty of nineteen who was as intrepid as her husband. Baroness Elisabeth Wrangell was the first wife to accompany her husband to his post and, like Irina Baranov, she was known for her gaiety, kindness, and charm. She was friendly and gracious with the Indian women, often exchanging handcrafts or tending the sick.

Ten-legged polar bear

Wrangell, distressed at the abuse of the fur animals in Russian America, believed in developing the country's other resources and in passing game conservation laws. This was a startling idea to most people, who could not foresee that animals might be totally wiped out unless there was sensible management.

When the Wrangells left Russian America in 1835, their son, born in America, was with them, but their little girl, who had died, was buried in Sitka. The Wrangells were lucky in their homeward trip. They returned to Russia by taking a ship to Mexico, going overland to the Atlantic Ocean, and catching another ship to New York. From there they took yet another ship to Europe, reaching St. Petersburg by coach. This journey took a matter of months rather than the years that it took to reach the Russian capital city from Alaska through Siberia. Such rapid travel was indeed a blessing!

Baron Wrangell's reports on declining fur animals stirred the Russian government to send an expedition to see what other treasures Russian America had to offer. In December, 1842, Naval Lieutenant Lavrentiy Zagoskin, a hardy 34-year-old Russian explorer, and five companions

"Walrus," painted by Kivetoruk Moses

Whale carving

arrived in northern Alaska, ready to investigate the unmapped interior of Russia's American holdings. The midwinter darkness of the frozen Arctic did not deter this exceptional group of scientists, who set out with dog teams over the ice to look for the headwaters of the Yukon and Kuskokwim rivers. All that was known to Russia about the area was that these two great rivers emptied into the Bering Sea. For one-and-a-half years the group hiked, packed, and studied, traveling by canoe, dog team, and snow shoes, where no Europeans had ever been before. Zagoskin's .journals, now translated into English, left a unique record of the Athapascan Indians and the unspoiled land of early Alaska.

While Lieutenant Zagoskin was getting ready to set out on the historic journey, he spent some time of preparation in the company's headquarters at Sitka. A careful writer, he noted in vivid detail how the Russian colonists lived. He attended a masquerade ball for 150 people at the Christmas season, but the social event that meant most to him was the children's party held at the house of the company manager, an annual New Year's event.

There was a Christmas tree ablaze with candles for the twenty children of the Russian employees. There were candies and nuts and glittering toys sent from Russia, so that the Russian American children would not lose their traditional Christmas and New Year's links with their parents' homeland.

The Russians certainly had the first Christmas trees in Alaska, at a period when the custom was not general in the United States. The Russians who had moved to Alaska had little reason to believe that their thriving culture in North America would soon not only be gone but almost forgotten, simply a footnote in the history of the United States of America.

12 ❖❖❖

The Natives Fight Back

WHILE the Russians were placing copper plates to warn other European explorers to keep out of the territory extending from the Aleutian Islands onto mainland Alaska, how did the Aleuts, the Indians, and the Eskimos feel? The Native people had no written language to record their emotions, but there were oral accounts and historical events to give a picture of their side. In general they hated the Russian invaders and fought back. They suffered from new diseases, the impact of new ideas, warfare, slavery, and the loss of their fishing and hunting lands. They were gradually forced into a new way of life, using a money exchange instead of the old system of barter. Yet the Russians were kind as well as cruel, and some of the changes were beneficial as well as destructive.

The historian Hubert Howe Bancroft tells a firsthand tale from an old man, Arsenti Aminak, whose story of his childhood was written down word for word by a translator on Kodiak long ago. It happened in about 1760 when Aminak, a Kodiak Native, was a little boy of ten or so. He had never seen a ship with sails, although his people paddled to other islands and the mainland in their open skin boats. When he spied a sailing vessel on the horizon the people thought it was a great whale and ran to the water in curiosity. Soon they discovered that it was not a whale, but an unknown monster that filled them with fear.

78

A Russian soldier

Many of them ran and hid, but curiosity brought them back to the shore. Aminak recalled that one brave man, Ishinik, was so bold that he feared nothing in the world. He visited the ship and touched the men on it and found out that they wished to trade skins for beads. Yet the elders feared these strange white men with their odd clothes, not believing they had come in friendship. The elders were right. While the trading was taking place, some Aleuts who had been enslaved by the Russians fell on the Kodiak people with guns and killed thirty of them. The Russians then seized the skins, and Aminak and the others who survived escaped in their small boats to safer places.

The Russians stayed at Kodiak for the winter, living in tents. They raided other communities, stealing food and skins, while the Natives fled to the hills. Once, Aminak remembered, he secretly watched in glee as the hungry Russians ate poisonous starfish. The fish were so deadly that even the sea gulls would not touch them, but the Russians did not know this. The Indians had no guns to fight with so they thanked the gods of nature for helping them destroy the invaders by this accidental means.

Most of the stories of the Native heroes have not been recorded, but one celebrated confrontation took place at Sitka where Manager Baranov had decided to build a strong fort and a new settlement to be the Russian American headquarters. Many Indians were already living there, and when they heard of Baranov's plan they angrily got ready to defend their property. In July, 1799, the Indians entrenched themselves on a high point and silently watched the Russians arrive in their canoes.

The Russians were busily cutting trees so they could build a fort in a lower spot when about twenty tall, solemn Native warriors filed out from the forest with Chief Ska-out-lelt in the lead. Over their shoulders they wore handsome wool blankets, woven with tribal designs. Some of them carried guns.

Baranov laid down his ax and stepped forward with dignity, and made a speech, in the Native tongue, saying that they had come in friendship to trade, and they wished to buy the land where they would put a trading post. The Russians would protect the Indians from other White men who had treated them badly in the past. The Indians said nothing. Finally the chief asked how much the Russians would pay. After a parley the Russians bought the land, and for a short time there was peaceful trading, for the Indians wanted the goods that the Russians had to offer.

All through the winter a thousand Russians worked on their new settlement and fortifications. The fortress was strong and built to withstand a siege, with a high log palisade surrounding it. The air was uneasy, for the Russians found out that the Sitka chief was criticized by other Indian clans for selling the land to the Russians. There might be an uprising among these warlike people.

Early print of the harbor of Sitka (New Archangel), 1805

On Easter Sunday the Russians had a festive ceremony, in spite of the strain. In the midst of it the Indians kidnapped one of the Russian interpreters. Baranov coolly finished the Easter service and then, in the midst of hundreds of unsmiling Indians, he marched to the chief and demanded the return of the prisoner while guns were fired overhead. The kidnapped Russian was returned, but peace was not restored.

Firearms were coming into the area from American ships which brought old Revolutionary War guns to trade. When Baranov departed in the summer of 1800 to return to his family in Kodiak, he left a garrison of 450 of his people, hunters and their wives, among the Indians.

Bad luck for the Russians was good luck to the Natives. For four years no supply ship came from Russia so there was little trading. Finally in 1802 a ship arrived. Word was sent for men to bring furs from Sitka to Kodiak for shipment to Russia, so there were fewer people and the discipline was relaxed in the fort at Sitka. There was a holiday air about the place. At this moment of apparent peace the Indians struck. A few Russians and their Aleut or Indian wives and children escaped to tell

Tlingit Indian house post totem

Yakutat Indian house rain screen

tales of violence and torture. The survivors were picked up by a British ship and brought to Kodiak for ransom.

The raid had been actually led by Kotlean, the old chief's nephew. Retaking Sitka from Kotlean and his warriors became the obsession of Baranov's life. He was determined to make Sitka a Russian stronghold at any cost.

In 1804, Baranov arrived at the rotting, deserted ruins of the Russian fortress at Sitka, his mind and plans set at nothing less than destroying the Indian fortress on the hill. This time he had a Russian warship in the harbor as well as other supporting ships. Baranov planted a flag on the place he originally had named New Archangel.

**Haida Indian maskette,
ceremonial head ornament**

Totem pole

There was an attempt at negotiations, but in the end the Russians battered down the last Indian stronghold, after bitter, bloody fighting. In October, 1804, the Indians gave up under the superior forces and weapons of the Russians. All night there was a fearful chanting. When the Russians entered the vanquished stockade, they found it piled with dead bodies, many of them children whose parents had preferred to kill them rather than to let them fall into Russian hands.

Chief Kotlean is an Alaskan hero, for he fought bravely in his vain effort to hold onto his people's land. Today in Sitka the United States National Park Service has a 54-acre park at the battle site commemorating the last stand of the Sitka Indian warriors.

13 ❖❖❖

Rebel Yells in the Bering Sea

A LITTLE more than two centuries after the first Russian explorers came to North America, the Civil War was raging in the United States. The Russians paid little attention to the faraway war, even though Yankee whaling ships were operating in Russian American waters. The Confederate Navy took note.

Lieutenant James Waddell of the Confederacy decided that his ship, the *Shenandoah,* could help his cause by sinking Yankee ships bringing whale oil to New England.

The *Shenandoah* was a sharp ship, built in England and guaranteed to be fast and dependable, for she had both sails and steam. Setting out from Europe, the Confederates sailed to the South Atlantic Ocean, around the Cape of Good Hope, and into the Indian Ocean, capturing whalers, seizing the cargoes, and putting captives ashore at the nearest island before burning the ship. After a series of captures in the South Pacific, the raiders headed north toward Russian America.

Near Kamchatka, opposite Alaska, they sank more vessels, and by June, 1865, they entered the Bering Sea. Waddell didn't know that the Civil War was already over and that the Confederates had surrendered.

Overwhelmed by success, the *Shenandoah,* under full steam and sail, went after Yankee whalers. Near the Aleutians they captured the whaler

Confederate raider *Shenandoah* towing prisoners from burning whalers, 1865

William Thompson, and a few hours later they sighted more sails and captured the ship *Euphrates.* They took some of the crew aboard as prisoners, put some ashore, and burned the ships. The Yankee whalers groaned in agony and astonishment, and the Confederates sent rebel yells bounding over the Bering Sea. Two captures in one day! They were indeed "whistling Dixie."

Heading north, they took another ship the following day.

"But the war is over," pleaded the captain.

"Impossible," said Waddell curtly. His success had been so great he was sure the luck had turned for the entire South.

In the next few weeks the *Shenandoah* captured and burned twenty more Yankee whaling vessels in Russian American waters. On June 29 she passed through the Bering Strait into the Arctic Ocean itself but, the ice being too heavy for a long voyage there, she turned south.

Meantime some of the Yankee prisoners had escaped in small boats, and the alarm was sounded that a mad raider was at large. By mid-July

Another old print of the Confederate raider _Shenandoah_

the _Shenandoah_ was out of the Bering Sea, headed for California. On one of the captured ships Waddell had found a newspaper that told of the fall of the Confederacy.

"I suppose you might say we're in 'hot water,' even though we are in the north," said one crew member, trying to make a joke in a grim situation.

"What'll we do now?" the officers asked each other.

"Our war isn't over," said Lieutenant Waddell. "The _Shenandoah_ is going to capture the city of San Francisco."

Actually, San Francisco was not well protected, and the inhabitants were afraid that the city could be taken, for stories of the _Shenandoah_ had spread up and down the Pacific coast. The United States Navy was alerted to capture "the rebel pirates," as they were being called.

The raid on San Francisco didn't take place. Waddell was warned by a British ship that the United States Navy would surely catch him. At last he believed it. Sadly, the raiders took down the Confederate flag, hid the guns, whitewashed the ship, and headed as quietly as possible for England, hoping that nobody would stop and question them. When the *Shenandoah*, with no name or flag showing, slipped into Liverpool harbor in England, the Confederate Navy had been around the world!

The *Shenandoah*, which Waddell turned over to the American consul, had captured thirty-eight United States vessels worth nearly one and a half million dollars and had taken over one thousand prisoners. Lieutenant James Waddell and his shipmates decided they had better stay in Europe for a while. After the war-feeling had subsided at home, Waddell went back to his own country and even went back to sea on United States merchant ships, no doubt spinning sea stories of the Dixie victory in the Bering Sea.

Russian American waters were the scene of the last shots fired in the Civil War, even though the war was over, but the exploits of the *Shenandoah* had an unexpected effect on all of America. The United States realized that, with her westward expansion, she needed a strong Pacific fleet and ports for ships, and a few farsighted people in the government began to look uneasily at the Russian colony not very far north of California.

14 ❖❖❖

The Telegraph Tale

IN 1861 the east and west coasts of the United States were linked by telegraph wires that could carry messages as fast as sound could travel. People were even thinking of circling the entire world with this almost instant communication.

Meantime, the isolated Russians in Alaska had a special problem of their own: the Russian government did not renew the charter for the Russian American Company. Uneasily, the colonial Russians wondered about their future.

Down in San Francisco there were Americans eager to be involved in Russian trade. A new organization called the American Russian Company had been sending ships to Alaska for the last ten years to buy ice, of all things, for the gold-rich people of California. The United States was moving steadily closer to Russian America, and then, in 1864, newcomers literally slipped into the colony's back door. News spread that the Yankees were going to build a telegraph line that would link America to Siberia and St. Petersburg and the rest of Europe!

The story of the east-to-west telegraph line began with an enterprising American businessman, scientist, and inventor—Perry Collins. Cyrus Field had tried over and over to lay a telegraph cable across the Atlantic Ocean to bind Europe and America but, even when he got one across in 1858, it didn't carry the sound properly.

Travel by dog sled in the rugged Arctic

Collins thought he could get messages to Europe another way. A man with a broad horizon, he had been to Russia and traveled across rugged Siberia for two years. He knew what he was talking about when he went to the Western Union Telegraph Company with a proposition that was so fantastic that the officials were flabbergasted.

"Why can't we link Europe and America by way of Asia? At the Bering Strait in Russian America there are only fifty-five miles of water to cross. Why not run the telegraph lines north from San Francisco, through British Columbia, and across Russian America, and under the Bering Strait to Siberia?"

Collins pulled out a map and excitedly traced his route with his forefinger. "Meanwhile the Russians could run a line from St. Petersburg across Siberia to meet it. St. Petersburg is already connected with the rest of Europe by telegraph wires. We could even hook up with China near the Siberian border—can't you see, it could be the most important project the world has ever undertaken!" Collins might have said.

The Western Union corporation officers looked at the map and nodded their heads. It just might work, and think of the riches if they could carry European news over sixteen thousand miles of wire from east to west, rather than from west to east as the rival cable company was trying to do.

In spite of the Civil War, Collins got company and government backing for the project. Then he set out again for Russia, this time to persuade their officials to join the international telegraph scheme. In 1863, Russia agreed, and the following year Great Britain said the line could go through her British Columbia territory.

In 1865, the Civil War had just ended and Collins was ready to begin the work. He knew that Western Union would have to hurry to get its line laid before Cyrus Field succeeded in laying the Atlantic cable.

Collins' project was divided into three sections: one group was to get the line from San Francisco through British Columbia; the second team was to work from St. Petersburg through Siberia; and the third crew was to lay a line through the wild interior of Russian America to meet the second party at the Bering Strait.

Robert Kennicott, a gifted young naturalist still in his twenties, was chosen to head the Russian American division. It took rugged young men to endure the hardships of this cold-weather project. Kennicott had explored some of this area earlier for the Smithsonian Institution and the Chicago Academy of Sciences. He was bursting with enthusiasm to get back into the country where there were species of birds and flowers and minerals and animals that were unknown in the United States. He wanted to explore rivers and mountains and see country that White men had never visited.

Kennicott was a loner who disliked corporations as much as he liked the outdoors. He was a man of science, but his job required him to be a business executive. However, Kennicott got permission to hire six other naturalists to work with him. He called them the Western Union Scientific Corps, and he himself headed the Scientific Corps as well as the Russian American division of the telegraph project.

The seven naturalists were given uniforms, which Kennicott despised, and a flag that he felt was silly, but those were only minor irritations compared with his real problems. He felt that the route chosen by the Western Union Company from the Fraser River and along the Yukon was the wrong choice. He had favored using the Mackenzie River, which he had explored previously. Furthermore, the steamer that was to bring supplies on the

The Natives looked upon the telegraph crews as lunatics. Eskimo dolls.

Yukon River did not operate properly and was smashed on the rocks. There wasn't enough food nor enough sled dogs. There was petty jealousy among the scientists.

The Indians and Eskimos who were in contact with these White men looked upon them as lunatics and were not in the least interested in working for them. However, a Native Creole, Simon Lukeen, was different. He was caught up in the romance of exploration and communication and helped the strangers.

Although the scientific explorations and the work on the telegraph lines were moving forward, Kennicott was depressed and overworked. One morning he morbidly wrote a note of instructions of what to do in case of his death. It was spring, a time of joy in the north. Kennicott walked away from the camp near the Russian outpost of Nulato on the Yukon River, and when he failed to return his friends went out to look

Two drawings by William Dall, Athapascan Indians and fur seals

An early view of Sitka by Frederick Whymper

for him. They found him dead, apparently of a heart attack. Sadly they buried him. Over his head they placed a marker:

> In Memory of Robert Kennicott, Naturalist
> Who died near this place on May 13, 1866, age 30.

In the summer of that year the Atlantic cable was finally laid, connecting Europe and America, but the workers in the interior of Russian America did not know this. Soon after Kennicott died, his friend and colleague William Dall arrived to join the Scientific Corps. Dall took over the leadership with a heavy heart. But he got the poles cut and raised for the wires that were scheduled to arrive soon.

The explorers separated into smaller teams and, in the winter of 1866–1867, Dall and the artist Frederick Whymper stayed at Nulato. It was so cold that the artist's fingers froze along with the water when he tried to work with water colors.

When the weather warmed and ice began to move, so did the mosquitoes. The men were nearly eaten alive. In July word reached the

Scientific Corps that they should return to St. Michaels. There the men discovered that the cable had been laid across the Atlantic a year before! Their project was to be immediately abandoned—in defeat.

But 22-year-old William Dall was not about to be defeated. Like young Georg Stellar a century before, he had been overwhelmed with the natural wonders of Alaska. When Dall decided to stay on and continue his work as a scientist, he persuaded the Western Union Company to give him his back wages in groceries. He managed to get a little financial help from the Smithsonian Institution, and he returned to the interior to live among the Indians.

On February 3, 1868, Dall was at the Russian log fort at Nulato when he heard a great commotion of people and dogs arriving. Company was an exciting event in this cold, remote spot. The visitor was Simon Lukeen, who was obviously bursting with news for his friend. Dall had to coax him for a while to find out what it was.

Finally Lukeen could hold it no longer. "The United States has bought Russian America," he blurted out. "This has been United States territory for almost a year now!"

Dall leaped to his feet with a rush of patriotism. "Come on, Simon. Let's prove it." And William Dall raised the Stars and Stripes over the old Russian fort at Nulato while the Indians and Creoles in the settlement looked on stoically. What would this man think of next? He filled his room with worthless bones and bugs and twigs; he spent his time writing and drawing. Now he was in a frenzy of excitement about running up a new flag.

15 ❖❖❖

Alaska Under the Americans: Should Polar Bears Vote?

W HEN the United States acquired Alaska, American citizens, not knowing much about the area, seemed to take a lighthearted interest in the new possession.

Should polar bears vote? That was the kind of humor that ran through the press after the news of the purchase was announced in 1867. The Civil War was just over and people wanted something to be happy about. Poking fun at "America's icebox," as some called it, was just what they seemed to relish. But it wasn't funny to everybody, for the lives of the people in Alaska were dreadfully upset.

Many people wondered why Russia wanted to sell her North American land. Probably it was because Russian government officials felt that they could not protect this far-flung colony if another nation decided to seize it.

The sale of Russian America had been brewing for some years, and probably would have taken place sooner if the war in the United States had not kept Congress too busy to think about such matters as buying more real estate. United States Secretary of State William F. Seward, a man of determination and foresight, knew that Russia was willing to sell and worked hard to persuade Congress that Russian America was worth the $7,200,000 price tag.

Even though there were almost 600,000 square miles in the package, most of the lawmakers in Washington had difficulty realizing that this was a bargain, about $12.00 a square mile—a few cents an acre. However, they finally agreed, grumbling about "Seward's Folly"; and the newspapers had even more fun writing about what they called "Walrussia" because of the many walruses in Alaska.

The treaty of transfer was concluded on March 30, 1867. Although Dall and the Western Union Scientific Corps had received their orders to abandon the telegraph project in July because the Atlantic cable had been successfully laid, the Western Union work in Alaska had great influence on the sale, for firsthand news from the telegraph workers concerning Alaska reached the United States just when the purchase was being considered. Some of the men from the Western Union Scientific Corps had gone to Congress to testify about the value of this wild interior.

On October 18, 1867, at three-thirty in the afternoon, a formal ceremony of transfer took place at Sitka. Three United States ships were in the harbor. General Lovell Rousseau accepted the land for his country as the Russian flag was lowered in front of the residence of the chief manager. The Imperial Russian flag didn't want to come down: it caught in the ropes, and someone had to climb the flagpole and cut it down. It was a sad moment for the uniformed Russians who stood at solemn attention as the flag of the United States was raised.

The last chief manager of Russian America was a nobleman, Prince Dmitri Maksoutoff, who stood with his princess beside him as Russia formally ended her two centuries of domination in this corner of North America. The princess wept, but there is no record that American soldiers cared much one way or another.

There was at first a real problem about what to call the new place. Maps of the period simply labeled it Russian-America, which obviously was not going to be suitable any more. The Aleuts had always referred to the mainland as Aleyska, and the long peninsula that extends southwest toward the Aleutian Islands was usually called the Alaska Peninsula.

Signing the treaty of transfer of Russian America to the United States

So despite suggestions that the new purchase be called "Alexanderland" in honor of the friendly Russian Emperor, or "Yukon" after the river, or "Seward" in honor of the Secretary of State, or "Sitka" or "Aleutia" or any of a number of other ideas, Alaska was the name that finally stuck. The name seems to have been assumed by popular consent among newspapers and the general public. But like a baby without a name, the area was referred to as "the Russian purchase," even in official circles, for an embarrassingly long time as there seems to have never been a formal naming.

American merchants rushed in to buy the furs and other goods owned by the old Russian American Company. This was the beginning of the Alaska Commercial Company which was to have a long life. American merchant ships took the things away soon after the transfer ceremony at Sitka.

The treaty said that the Russians in Alaska had three years to decide if they wanted to become citizens of the United States, but this right was not offered to the Native people who were specifically excluded. Most of the Russians chose to return to their homeland in the ships that came to carry them away, for they were uneasy about the prospect of life under the United States Army. American soldiers moved into the old Russian barracks in Sitka, the town that became American headquarters.

When the Russians left, law and order, schools, churches, courts, and protection of property went too. Alaska was called a "customs district," with Sitka being the only port where goods could legally be shipped in and out. Since the handful of soldiers was the only law enforcement agency, smuggling was open and defiant.

At least one Russian became an American citizen, and at least one Aleut was happy at the change. An old man from Unalaska Island in the Aleutians said that he liked the Americans better than the Russians because the Americans left the Natives alone, giving them a chance to get back to their old way of life. That was all that was said in favor of the new administration. It was agreed that the American government neglected Alaska most dreadfully, and when bored soldiers taught some local Indians how to make liquor or "hootchinoo," the situation became quite serious for all concerned.

In spite of the efforts of some dedicated people, such as the customs collector and some of the military men, there were many problems with and among the Indians. In the year following the purchase there was a wave of witch-hunting among the Indians, and it was reported that, inspired by their medicine men, about one hundred Indians were executed by their own people for witchcraft. Probably the white man's liquor was partly to blame. There was slavery among the Indians too, a practice that was stopped by the Americans before long, for the Civil War had ended slavery in all its possessions. Things got steadily worse with fights

100

and killings, and no courts for justice. After ten years the Army was withdrawn and the American Navy was assigned to govern Alaska.

The Navy was able to govern since they had ships to take officials to the coastal settlements. There was little communication with the interior, for there were no roads, and there were still shameful incidents between Whites and Natives. Nobody was making jokes about Alaska then. "Alas, Alaska," said some newspapers. "Abandon Alaska," said others.

But some good things developed for and in Alaska in the last qaurter of the 1800's. A number of naturalists, scientists, explorers, and missionaries—men and a few women who were dedicated to the land, the people, and the future of Alaska—visited and wrote reports about the great land. One book could not list them all.

Since the United States did not provide any schools in its new possession for a long time, missionaries of many denominations opened church schools and boarding homes for Native children. Missionary societies in America sent money and supplies to help.

Russian-born Ivan Petroff conducted the first census in Alaska, the Tenth United States Census, in 1880. He gathered reams of material from all kinds of sources and recorded that Alaska had 33,426 people, of whom 430 were White.

In spite of increasing knowledge about Alaska, it remained a mystery land not taken very seriously. It was when early efforts were made to allow Alaskans to vote that one newspaper made a joke of it with the question, "Should polar bears vote?"

16 ❖❖❖

From Glaciers to Gold, and
the Story of a Brave Dog

WHEN Scottish-born John Muir came to Alaska, he was a well-known naturalist and writer, filled with an energy and inner glow that made others share his special way of looking at the wilderness.

People who believe in strong fate—and many Alaskans do—like to think that the meeting of Presbyterian missionary Samuel Hall Young and John Muir was meant to be. Young was a recent arrival at his mission post in Fort Wrangell in southeast Alaska, where he was to become a famous and trusted friend and teacher of the Indians. He met the red-bearded Muir one July day in 1879 when the naturalist stepped off the ship from California with a pack on his back, bound for adventures in Alaska.

Both were new to this mysterious land and wanted to learn about it. They quickly became close friends and together boarded a steamer with some visiting missionaries and went up the Stikeen River. The eager young missionary and the naturalist stood breathless on the deck, looking at glaciers. When the ship had to anchor until a strong wind died down, they left the ship and made a rush for the mountains.

Running and scrambling, for they had little time, they were determined to see the sunset from the highest peak. Young fell upside down

Glaciers and snow fields seen from the air.

into a crevasse, or crack, in the glacier they were crossing, and Muir rescued him in a seemingly impossible feat of courage and skill. Both of Young's shoulders were dislocated and he had faced death as he looked down the thousands of feet below while he dangled in the crevasse. When he returned half dead to the ship, his body was battered but his spirit was fully alive with the miracle of glaciers. Immediately the two men began planning a trip to explore the legendary bay of frozen rivers that lay to the north.

It was October, dangerously late weather in cold Alaskan waters, before Muir and Young could set out from Fort Wrangell, this time in canoes with Indian helpers. (The reason for the delay was that Young's wife had been expecting their first baby, and the father waited until their daughter was born.) Provided with tents and food and guns, but no maps, for this was uncharted water, they headed north on the inland passage on their 800-mile, six-week trip. Young made stops to minister to the

Indians along the way while Muir made notes and sketches of people and places that were new to him.

On October 24 they entered the place now called Glacier Bay. None of them, Whites or Indians, had ever seen such splendor as the deep blue and sparkling white of the glaciers unfolding before them while rain, snow, mist, and fog made changing vistas. Today Muir Glacier in Glacier Bay National Monument is one of the great sights of the State of Alaska.

In 1880, the two glaciologists, with Indian friends from Fort Wrangell to help them, returned to Glacier Bay for more exploration. Muir was in the canoe, ready to go, when Young hurried through the crowd that had gathered to see them off, his little mongrel dog, Stikeen, at his heels.

"You can't bring your dog," said Muir impatiently. But Young and the dog climbed in.

"Oh, Stikeen will be a great companion," said Young, stroking the dog's head affectionately. The Indians were already paddling away from the docks.

"No, no," insisted Muir. "Pass the dog back to the children there." But Stikeen had curled up in the bottom of the canoe, defying anyone to send him back. The paddlers grinned and worked faster. They wanted the dog along for he was considered a lucky mascot.

Muir soon fell under the spell of this determined little dog that immediately adopted Muir as his master. Stikeen liked adventures. He would lie quietly in the bottom of the canoe, but he was always aware if there was danger or special excitement ahead. He would rouse himself and look at Muir as if to say, "Get ready, something is about to happen!"

When Stikeen heard the men talking of going ashore he would jump over the side and swim ahead. Once ashore he would run into the bush to hunt for food for himself. Although he was the first to leave the boat, he was the last to come aboard. He would not come at anybody's call, but when the boat was shoving off, out would bound Stikeen, swimming alongside, begging to be lifted into the canoe.

Stikeen would never let Muir out of his sight for fear he might miss

Alaska's dogs still like to play on the ice as Stikeen did.

some great adventure. The dog especially liked romping on glaciers with his master. One gusty morning very early, Muir, who loved storms, rose quietly in his tent and tried to slip out of camp alone to watch the rising fury. Ignoring breakfast and tiptoeing over his sleeping friends, he set off. Before long he realized that Stikeen was frisking along at his heels.

"Go, go back," ordered Muir, quite outdone. But Stikeen stuck right by his friend. He was bound for adventure, and no orders would make him turn back. As the storm grew more intense, Muir and Stikeen found shelter under some trees. Finally they ventured onto the glacier.

The ice was smooth at first, but soon they were weaving their way among small ice cracks which Stikeen leaped over merrily. Suddenly snow began to blind both man and dog, making it impossible to see the dangerous cracks in the thick ice. Finally they found themselves trapped: the only way out was to make narrow ice steps on the face of a cliff, a situation only a skilled mountain climber can understand. By using his ice ax and inching his way with absolute balance, Muir knew he had a chance to save himself, but what about Stikeen?

Muir stopped and considered. He would have to rely on Stikeen's supernatural powers. Muir began to move ahead, cutting the steps in the ice, and for the first time in his life Stikeen began to cry, really cry like a person in terrible agony. Finally Muir made his way across to safety, but Stikeen stood on the opposite brink wailing.

Muir leaned toward him and called encouragement. Finally Stikeen began to grow calm, and Muir gave the dog directions to show him how to climb down and then up in Muir's footsteps. He literally talked Stikeen across the crevasse as the dog dug his claws into the narrow ice steps. Muir held his breath as the little dog inched his way to safety. When Stikeen's paws finally reached Muir's side, Muir sat back with a deep sigh of relief, but Stikeen went wild with joy. He ran in circles, barking and leaping. He seemed to be trying to shout, "Saved, saved!" and to thank John Muir for his life.

John Muir's scientific observations and learned papers about glaciology have been important, but his story of Stikeen, which he told many times and wrote for the old and young of his day, probably touched more people.

On both journeys Muir and Young stopped to explore the great glacier (now called the Mendenhall Glacier, at the town of Juneau) near the home of the Auk Indians. While Missionary Young preached to the Auks, naturalist Muir noticed that there was gold in the rocks and streams of the area. Neither of the men was interested in the glitter of gold for personal wealth, but Muir casually mentioned the gold a few weeks later as he waited in Sitka for the ship that would take him home to California.

Gold? Ears were alert, for there were prospectors in Sitka who had drifted over from British Columbia where there had been a gold stampede a few years before. Muir's words were picked up by an engineer who sent a pair of roving miners, Joe Juneau and Dick Harris, to look over the area. Harris and Juneau did find the gold. That was the beginning of the first big mining operation in Alaska and of Juneau, the first new town built under the Americans. The 1880 gold rush turned the attention of the world to the riches of the new American possession.

17 ❖❖❖

Men with Picks and Packs

THEY took their picks and packs and headed for Alaska to seek their fortunes. In the 1880's most of the few white people in Alaska were prospectors looking for gold. The land belonged to everybody, and the only laws were the informal "miners' meetings" that sometimes banished those who misbehaved. Some people were literally run out of the country.

But people kept on arriving, lured by the Juneau find which was on its way to becoming the largest gold-mining operation in the world. The Congress back in Washington finally passed some laws in 1884 giving Alaska a governor, appointed by the President, and some courts and judges. The missionaries were given a small sum to run a school system for Whites and Natives, and the mining laws of the United States were put into effect.

To stake a mining claim a person who found gold would put stakes on the four corners of the find, which could not exceed twenty acres total, with his name and the discovery date on the stakes. Within ninety days he had to do some work on the land he had staked, and he had to record his find with a government agency. Each year he had to prove that he was working the land to hold his claim.

The air was heavy with dreams of gold. Rumors went around that real nuggets were to be found beyond the mountains in Canada's Yukon, and

Photo of "Prospector," mosaic tile, courtesy of Behrends Department Store, Juneau, Alaska

that a man named Holt had found gold beyond belief before he had been killed by the Indians. For as long as anybody remembered the passes through the forbidding mountains had been guarded by the Indians for their fur trade, but finally the Indians had been persuaded to let miners go through the passes near the present town of Skagway.

So a trickle of prospectors reached the interior of Alaska and Canada one way or another, and there were small gold rushes in the land where Canada's Yukon Territory and Alaska lie side by side. (It was 1903 before the border was firmly established, after some squabbling by the governments of the two countries.) Some farsighted traders began to move in.

The idea of fate and luck and the belief in dreams and omens that hung like a web over the Yukon area explained good and bad luck to the miners. In July, 1896, Robert Henderson, a lonely Canadian miner who had been looking for gold all his life, found some in a creek that fed into the Klondike River. There was not a lot, but it looked promising. He went to the nearest trading post to record his claim and spread the word, as that was the code of the miners. On the way back he ran into another prospector, George Carmack, who was standing by the stream bank where the Yukon and Klondike rivers meet.

Henderson stopped to tell Carmack about the gold. Carmack, on Henderson's advice, said he would look over a place called Rabbit Creek.

"Let me know if you find anything," said Henderson, and Carmack promised that he would.

Carmack had an Indian wife named Kate, and his two brothers-in-law, Skookum Jim and Tagish Charlie, were his best friends. He was close to the Indians, but Henderson was more aloof. After telling Carmack of the new find, Henderson added a few ill-chosen words: "But don't bring all those Indians with you."

Carmack and his Indian in-laws were peeved with that remark. After Henderson left, Carmack turned to his friends. "Let's try it, boys. I have a feeling I might have good luck."

He had dreamed that he caught a salmon with scales and eyes of gold, but at the time he'd thought the dream meant he should go fishing. That was what he was doing when Henderson stopped to share his news. He was fishing for a golden salmon!

Carmack, Charlie, and Jim took a leisurely hike over to Rabbit Creek the next day, and there they found gold, more gold than anyone could have imagined, on the richest few feet of earth in the world. Rabbit Creek, which was renamed Bonanza, soon became known all over the globe.

Lumps of pure gold were there—raw, thick, as dreamlike as a gold-scaled salmon. But this was real. They ran their hands through it, screamed, shouted, danced, and staked three claims, one each as the law provided. But they didn't tell Henderson, who was just across the mountain. They broke the unwritten law of the prospectors. Henderson never recovered from his bitter resentment, for by the time the word got to him about the discovery, all the good land was claimed.

The Seattle paper of July 17, 1897, announced to the world that "a ton of gold" was on its way out of the Yukon. Men with "pokes of gold" were coming out to prove it, and the rush was on. The best way to get to the Klondike region was over the passes beyond the now booming town of Skagway, although some people tried the Yukon River from the old Russian town of St. Michaels. It is said that 100,000 people, men, women, and children, left their homes to try to reach that land of gold.

Uprooted humanity crowded into the trains to the West Coast, where they fought, bought, and cheated to get on ships. They'd sail on anything that would float, to take them, and their pack animals if they could get them, to Alaska. There they would begin the real trial of the trail, packing and transporting mining supplies and food for a dangerous trip and unpredictable life ahead. Most of them were ill prepared.

Shelves and shelves of books have been written about the "Great Stampede," and reams of old letters and journals are in libraries and museums and attics throughout America. Alaska especially abounds in stories about the great gold rush, true and false.

The little trading post of Skagway grew overnight into a bedlam of thousands, with few houses, little food, and mass confusion. Sometimes there were twelve thousand people there competing for the space and supplies. The old-time prospectors were called "sourdoughs" because they lived chiefly on bread made with fermented dough, still a staple of the north. The Indians called the newcomers "cheechakos," a term still used today to distinguish new arrivals from earlier settlers in Alaska.

Some people found their fortune in running trading posts, laundries, and hotels. Others got gold by working as packers or selling food. Harriet Pullen struck it rich making apple pies for hungry miners in Skagway.

Law and order were lacking. One "Soapy" Smith was said to have made his money by controlling a gang that stole the gold of successful

Monument to the pack animals on White Pass

miners as they reached the end of the outbound trail. Soapy was killed in a celebrated shoot-out with Frank Reid, who also died in the duel.

Ministers and doctors came to aid people, and writers, photographers, entertainers, and speculators of all kinds joined the crowd. Mostly it was not a pretty story, for it was largely built on greed. It was a sad story, too, for it was also built on need. Times were desperately hard all over America then, and many men and women saw in the gold fields the chance of a lifetime to get out of debt. More often than not they failed. In spite of problems there was real comradeship, courage, and a new kind of life with adventures enough for generations to spin yarns upon.

The two routes to the gold fields from Skagway, the Chilkoot and the White passes, were both dangerous and overcrowded. Some people tried to carry their loads on their backs, and the trails were littered with the things that they abandoned when the weight grew unbearable. A few pulled sleds by hand. Most tried to get pack animals such as oxen, horses, or mules. Mules were considered much the best and sold for outlandish prices.

Gold miners on the Chilkoot Pass

If a packed animal fell off the narrow, steep trail, he and his owner were often pushed aside, resulting in probable death and certain despair. Sometimes the animals were overloaded and abused.

So many mules and horses were killed on the White Pass that it was called Dead Horse Trail. Soon a railroad, which can still be ridden today, was built over the White Pass, and there is a monument on the old trail to the mules that died hauling freight.

One man who objected to the abuse of animals was John Feero, who arrived in Skagway in 1897. Taking a job with a packing agency, Feero demanded changes when he saw at the end of the first day that the mules were overworked and underfed. He proved that animals would work better with adequate food and kind treatment when his packtrain made the fastest journey on record. Feero and about a hundred others were killed in an avalanche on the Chilkoot Pass in the spring of 1898.

They were like chain gangs, the endless snakes of men and animals struggling up the mountains. If a man lost his place in the lines he might never get back in. Even after the passes were left behind the miners had to make long journeys by land and water to get to the place where a man could stake a claim to dig some gold-bearing gravel with his pick and shovel. Then he would wash out the mud, and with luck find gold in the pan. Those who did were just the fortunate few who had not starved, contracted scurvy or typhoid or other diseases, or died in violent accidents. Freezing and starvation were constant possibilities, and food and rent prices in the gold fields were beyond belief.

When the furor of the stampede of 1897 and 1898 had died down in the Yukon area, there were new Alaska gold rushes at Fairbanks, Nome, Valdez, and other places. Alaska had some real towns now; the spot where the Yukon and the Klondike met, the place where Carmack had fished for the gold salmon of his dreams, had become the town of Dawson.

In 1900 the population of Alaska was over sixty thousand, with about equal numbers of Whites and Natives. Salmon canning, copper mining, large-scale lumbering, commercial fishing—these and other industries slowly developed as Alaska began to take a more important part in the economy of America.

18 ❖❖❖

A Judge, a Myth, and a Mountain

IN 1900 there were eight times as many White people living in Alaska as there had been ten years before. Along with the newcomers came new problems. The Native people had held on to their ancient practices of law and justice, but there was bedlam among the Whites.

President William McKinley and Congress appointed James Wickersham of Tacoma, Washington, to be a federal judge. Judge Wickersham turned out to be the man for the job, and it was indeed a hard job. There was graft and dishonesty to be dealt with and there were all kinds of new problems that arose from mining claims and quarrels among the hordes

Mount McKinley

of prospectors. Not the least problem was the size of his district, 300,000 square miles.

Judge Wickersham's headquarters were at Eagle, just below the Arctic Circle near the Yukon border, and from there the new judge, with some new laws in his briefcase, would go into the wilderness to establish justice. The judge and his family arrived in Skagway by boat in July, 1900. The town had changed beyond recognition in the past two years. Now there was a real hotel, and the White Pass Railroad was completed to take them over the mountains to Whitehorse, where they boarded a Yukon River steamer for Dawson. From there they reached Eagle by canoe.

The new judge built his own moss-caulked log cabin and furniture. He bought a stove, cut some wood, and by the time the first snow fell the family were set for winter weather that was bound to be bitter.

"Expect 50 to 70 degrees below zero," they were warned by the few local inhabitants. There were no roads for getting around the huge district, so the hardy judge knew that his travels would be on foot, by dog sled, or canoe. He used all three, depending on the season.

Judge Wickersham spent the rest of his life in Alaska, serving as judge and as territorial delegate to Congress. He fought big corporations that tried to control the territory with unfair practices; he struggled for better

political status for Alaska, speaking out for statehood as early as 1916. Although he was trained as a lawyer, he became Alaska's well-known outdoorsman, writer, anthropologist, historian, and book collector as well. Trusted by the Native people, he learned and wrote down local customs as he dispensed justice.

He is remembered for all these things today, but many people think of him with most admiration when they realize that, at age forty-six, pretty old for a mountain climber, Judge Wickersham and four partners made the first known attempt to climb Mount McKinley, reaching an altitude of 8100 feet. Later Judge Wickersham, then a delegate to Congress, introduced the bill that created Mount McKinley National Park in 1917.

During his mountain climb in the summer of 1903 the judge sat around the campfire with his Indian friends listening to stories of Denali, the Great One, the Indian name for the highest (20,320 feet) mountain in North America. Today most Alaskans think of their great mountain as Denali, and there is a movement afoot to have the traditional name officially restored. (The name McKinley was given to Denali in 1897 by a mapper and surveyor who was happy that William McKinley had been nominated for the Presidency, totally ignoring the name that had been used as long as there had been people in Alaska.)

The blind chief Koonah, an Athapascan Indian, told the climbers the ancient story of how Denali was made. It began with Yako, the strong and handsome Indian shaman who had magic powers and plenty of game and everything he wanted, except a wife. The Great Bear told Yako that there were women of his tribe living with the people of another chief, Totson, the warrior. Yako made up his mind to go to that land and find a wife to share his life.

So Yako built a canoe and set out on the Yukon River to the land of Totson, where he arrived in a spirit of friendship, singing a song of peace. But Totson was jealous of the handsome young visitor and treated him rudely and sat back in his house, making plans to kill the newcomer.

The wife of the second chief was sorry for the young man. She went

Stained-glass window by Jessie Van Brunt at Holy Trinity

DENALI THE BIG CHIEF

to the river and whispered to Yako, "Take my daughter Tsukala. She is young, but she will grow up before long. Go quickly, for Totson is preparing to kill you."

The other women of the village were angry about this and tried to stop Tsukala from getting into the canoe. Yako stretched out his magic paddle and told the mother to put her daughter on it. Yako put the girl under the covering on his canoe just in time, for a magic wave came, killing all the jealous women. Only the mother of Tsukala escaped.

Totson now got into his canoe to chase Yako and Tsukala, hurling spears at them. Totson was a magician, too, and he made the waves grow stronger and higher, hoping to overturn Yako's canoe. But Yako's magic was greater for he had a lucky stone in his long black braid. Taking the rock from his hair, he threw it with all his strength toward his home.

The magic stone skipped ahead, leveling the sea so Yako could pass between Totson's violent waves. Totson kept on making the waves even larger and fiercer. Finally he gained on Yako until he could almost thrust a spear into his back. Yako saw the spear glisten as it arose.

With one mighty effort Yako brought out his best magic: he changed the oncoming wave into a mountain of stone! As Totson's spear rose higher and higher, all the waves reaching up were turned to stone as well. Totson's canoe struck against the rocks, and he was thrown against them. Instantly Totson was changed into a large black raven.

Yako had been stunned by the strain of his great magic. When he came to, he was in a forest ringed with snow-covered mountains. Tsukala, now grown into a beautiful woman, was preparing a supper of salmon and berries. Yako saw the spear of Totson shining from the highest peak and a raven flying overhead, crying to Yako to change him back to a warrior chief.

And there at the foot of Denali, the Great One, lived forevermore the descendants of Yako and Tsukala, the gentle Tena tribe of Athapascan Indians who never waged war.

This story must be true, for the shining snow-topped Denali sits in majesty in the midst of waves of smaller mountains that crowd around her feet for hundreds of miles.

19 ❖❖❖

Eight Stars of Gold on a Field of Blue

ALASKA became an official Territory of the United States in 1912, with an elected territorial legislature and a delegate in Congress. Juneau had been designated the capital city in 1906. With all these political steps taken, Alaska still had no flag.

Alaska's American Legion thought something ought to be done about it, because they knew that all the states and the other territories had flags displayed in Washington. But who would design the flag?

"Why don't we ask the children?" someone suggested. "After all, Alaska belongs to the future, so let the future citizens plan the flag."

So all the school children in Alaska from the seventh grade through high school were invited to enter the contest to make a flag for Alaska. In each town a local board of judges was set up, and everybody, old and young, was excited. The entries were to be in by March 1, 1927, and sent to Juneau for the final judging. Everybody wanted the prize, a gold watch with the winning design enameled on the back. The 1927 Legislature would make the award.

It seemed almost impossible to design one flag to represent the great variety of people, customs, land, water, and climate in the territory. Pictures ranging from polar bears to the aurora borealis that lights the sky at night were submitted. Gold panners, glaciers, totem poles, craggy

Bear motif is symbolic of Alaska.

mountains were offered. Nothing seemed to fit all the great land and all its people.

In those years many of the children in Alaska had to leave home to get an education if their villages were too small to support a school. Sometimes children lived in missionary boarding homes in order to attend a regional school. Such a person was Benny Benson, a motherless boy whose father had sent him to the Jesse Lee Mission Home when he was quite small. At thirteen, Benny was a seventh-grade pupil at the Seward Territorial School. A typical Alaskan, Benny's ancestry was Aleut, Russian, and Swedish.

Imagine owning a gold watch! Benny wanted to win the prize more than he had ever wanted anything in his life. I can't draw very well, he thought. But the rules said that it was the idea that counted most. The prize would go to the person who made a design that would have meaning to all Alaskans and would fit artistically on a flag.

Benny was a shy boy who loved the outdoors. He like to sit and look at the stars and feel the wind on his face and roam over the fields of flowers in the summer. It must have been the old Alaskan magic at work, for when the idea for his entry came to him all those things boiled up in his head and he saw it in his mind—a flag with the gold stars of the Big Dipper, and the eternal North Star, all on a field of sky-and-flower blue.

Hurriedly he took out a sheet of paper and began to sketch. Then he wrote down these words: "The blue field is for the Alaska sky and the forget-me-not, an Alaskan flower. The North Star is for the future state of Alaska, the most northerly in the union. The Dipper is for the Great Bear—symbolizing strength."

Benny won the contest. Both houses of the Territorial Legislature unanimously adopted his design and the American Legion Post in Seward presented him with the gold watch. Although there was considerable honor and attention brought to Benny, his proudest moment was on the

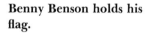

Benny Benson holds his flag.

**Modern-day Point Hope
Eskimo child**

day the flag, his flag, was raised for the first time on the flagpole at the Jesse Lee Home, the only home he had ever known, on July 10, 1927. He attached it himself to the halyards below the flag of the United States. Surrounded by his schoolmates, the local Boy Scouts, his teachers, and friends, he stood in the sunshine and with them sang the National Anthem and saluted the flag.

Later the Legislature voted to give Benny $1000 for his education. He used it to attend a vocational school and learned to be an airplane mechanic.

When Alaska became a state, the new Constitution made Benny

Benson's flag the official flag of the State of Alaska; and when it was flown over the Capitol of the new state in 1959, Benny, now a grown man, led the parade to the ceremony, carrying the flag that he had designed many years before.

When Benny Benson was growing old he gave the watch to the State Museum in Juneau so that all Alaskan children could enjoy seeing it. Beside it in the case is the original drawing he made of the flag. Many fine silk and wool flags of blue and gold fly today to show the world about Alaska and to remind children about the boy who won the contest by capturing on a flag forever his love of nature.

20 ❖❖❖

Highways, Wings, and War

EVEN after Alaska had a flag displayed in Washington, the Alaska Territorial Delegate to Congress had no vote. Alaskans felt that people in the "lower 48" didn't know or care much about the great land and her people. The only way to get in and out of Alaska was by ship, for there was no road or railroad to the outside. The people who controlled shipping controlled Alaska.

Alaskans looked up and saw their future in the air when the first Alaska air expedition of four planes from Mitchell Field in New York flew across the Territory to Nome in 1920. Four years later Colonel Carl Ben Eilson flew the mail on a 500-mile round trip from Fairbanks to McGrath on the Kuskokwim River. Dog teams running the same mail route took eighteen days. When that was compared with Eilson's nine-hour trip, Alaska began building airfields, and by 1932 there were a dozen commercial aviation companies operating in the Territory.

Brave bush pilots were pioneers with wings within Alaska, often landing on makeshift fields without navigational aids, but there were no scheduled airline flights to the outside world. More Alaskans have had private planes and pilots' licenses than any other group of people, considering the population. In spite of giant-sized hazards of snow, long darkness, rugged mountains, and isolated areas, Alaskans have used the

Light aircraft are used for remote areas.

air from the earliest days of aviation because most of the land has never been touched by roads.

In the 1920's and 1930's, citizens petitioned in vain for better transportation and communication, and the Delegate to Congress did his best to see that Alaska was not neglected. Thoughtful people along the Alaskan coast knew that Japanese fishing boats were always lurking in the local waters. Air-minded people realized that Alaska would one day be directly under the shortest air route between Europe and North America. World war was a real threat, and Alaska was almost totally undefended. There were plans for a strong Navy base in the Aleutians, but the government had never gotten around to building it.

"At least give us a highway to connect us with the rest of America," begged the people. But nothing happened until the bombing of Pearl Harbor in December, 1941, made Congress look at the map and see how easy it would be for the Japanese to seize Alaska.

Frantically, the United States and Canada realized there had to be a road, and fast! Work on the Alcan (now called the Alaska Highway) began

The Alcan Highway was pushed through unbelievable terrain during WWII.

in March, 1942. It took ten thousand men—soldiers and civilians, American and Canadian—fighting bitter cold in winter and blood-sucking mosquitoes in summer, to push that miraculous ribbon nearly two thousand miles through tough dirt, mountains of rocks, and dense forests. Everybody pitched in to make this an all-American highway, including French Canadians, Alaskan Indians, and a regiment of Black troops from the United States, working side by side. Men who were trying with all their strength to get the long overdue road built paused occasionally to say, "I like this place. When this war is over it would be a great adventure to drive this road."

And many did, settling in homesteads, especially in the fertile Matanuska Valley.

Before the highway was finished, Alaska got her first bitter taste of war at home. Military defenses had been started but they were too little and too late. The Japanese bombed Dutch Harbor on Unalaska Island in the Aleutians in June, 1942. Thanks to two small, secret, hastily constructed airfields in the area, American pilots were able to keep the enemy from landing, fighting them off while the Japanese made repeated attempts to seize their target. Within a few days, however, the Japanese occupied Attu and Kiska, two islands further down the Aleutian chain. Twenty-five hundred Japanese troops were landed on American soil, and the Americans and Canadians went to work to get the land back.

For over a year in 1942–1943, a brutal campaign was fought in Alaska's Aleutian Islands. Nearly half a million people took part, including American, Canadian, and Japanese. About 10,000 lives were lost; 2500 of them were Americans. Planes and ships went down by the score in the only campaign in North America in World War II. As the war in the Aleutians grew, 300,000 United States military persons were stationed in Alaska.

The Americans and their allies won back the Aleutians, moving down the island chain, building new bases from which to attack the entrenched enemy. When the Americans made their first full-scale amphibious landing in history in May, 1943, on Attu Island, it turned out to be the second most costly battle of the Pacific theater. On May 31, 1943, the Japanese conceded defeat, but there were four thousand American casualties, dead or wounded. Nobody had expected such a desperate struggle.

There was a happy surprise in store when American forces went ashore in Kiska in August, for the Japanese had evacuated the place. The troops had all been removed, mostly by submarine, and now the Aleutians were back in the hands of the United States.

While war tore at the Aleutians, exciting things were happening in other parts of Alaska. Governor Ernest Gruening was concerned about the northern Eskimos and about the great unknown miles of unprotected coast in the far north. The Governor had set up the Alaska Territorial Guard, and he wanted to have the Eskimos take part. He talked it over with his military aide, Major Marvin "Muktuk" Marston, who knew that

127

Eskimos were brave and resourceful people who could shoot straight and endure hardships.

A month after the Japanese bombed Pearl Harbor, Governor Gruening and Major Marston headed north to see if the Eskimos would like to join the Territorial Guard. They would and they did. "Muktuk" Marston's army became legendary in Alaska, although most of the world never heard of it. Eskimos flocked to the flag, and Major Marston was the man to lead them.

"Muktuk" Marston was no newcomer to the north. He had prospected in the northern bush, and he could drive a dog team and live in native style with ease. In the long dark winter of 1942, he and an Eskimo companion drove a dog team through the area, recruiting men to be lookouts and guards in the arctic guerrilla army with headquarters at Nome.

Although persons under sixteen were not supposed to be accepted, Eskimo boys were so eager to serve that even a few twelve-year-olds got in. Men of sixty were insulted if they were turned down for age, so just about all able-bodied Eskimos joined the "tundra army," as it was called. They would accept no pay, and to this day the Eskimo National Guard units protect the northernmost coast of North America.

Because of wartime security and censorship, few people know that there were many Russians in and out of Alaska during the war. Lend-lease planes were ferried from factories in the United States to Fairbanks. There Russian crews were ready to take the planes on trial runs to Nome and then on to the Soviet Union, crossing the Bering Sea to Siberia. In Nome the planes would wait for fair weather to take off. Many Alaskans remember those days when Russians were seen daily in Fairbanks and Nome, and once again the Russian tongue was heard freely in North America. Some of the pilots even brought wives and families to Alaska.

The Russian plane transfers in Alaska made Nome and Fairbanks likely targets for Japanese attack, and Eskimo lookouts were alert for enemy planes. While they served in the American forces, Eskimos were opening new doors for themselves. In the past, White men often had tried

Jet planes service much of Alaska today.

to keep proud Eskimos segregated. "Muktuk" Marston objected to this.

When Alberta Schenck, an Eskimo teenager, told Major Marston that her people were made to sit in a separate place in the Nome movie theater, he advised her to write a letter to the paper about it. Spunky little Alberta did just that, making a public issue of discrimination against Eskimos. Her well-worded letter in the paper came to the attention of the Governor, and before long Eskimos sat where they pleased.

The war took a terrible toll, but it had some good results in making the people of Alaska know more about each other and in making the rest of the world know more about Alaska.

21 ❖❖❖

It Isn't Easy to Become a State

ALASKANS who lived through the last stirring years of the territorial period know that it isn't easy for a territory to become a state. In fact, if it had not been for a determined group of people, in and out of Alaska, they might have given up altogether. For forty years congresses and presidents had found every imaginable reason why Alaska should not become a state, although a majority of Alaskans voted that they wanted to join the Union.

"We're tired of being second-class citizens," people said to each other.

"We even have to clear immigration before entering the United States, as though we are aliens trying to sneak in the back door," added others hotly.

Finally enough Alaskans got so fighting mad that things began to happen.

"We'll write our own constitution," angry citizens decided in 1955. The Territorial Legislature agreed. Money was set aside and twenty-two electoral districts were set up so that delegates could be chosen to frame a constitution.

Alaskans had never been more stirred or felt closer to each other than during the seventy-five days of the Constitutional Convention at the University of Alaska in Fairbanks. The election of the delegates had been

The governor's mansion, Juneau

The Lynn Canal, Juneau

ALMANAC		
Saturday, January 3, 1958		
Daylight Today 5 Hrs. 44 Min.		
Sunrise 9:52 a.m. Sunset 2:56 p.m.		
High yesterday		12
Low last night		10

Anchorage Daily Times

READ BY ALASKANS EVERYWHERE

FORTY-FOURTH YEAR   PHONE 36201   ANCHORAGE, ALASKA, SATURDAY, JANUARY 3, 1959   12 PAGES   PRICE 10 CENTS

IKE SAYS: 'YOU'RE IN NOW'

Proclamation Creating State

WASHINGTON (AP) — The text of President Eisenhower's proclamation admitting Alaska as the 49th state of the union follows.

The White House
Admission of the State of Alaska into the Union
By the President of the United States of America
A Proclamation

Whereas the Congress of the United States by the act approved on July 7, 1958 (22 Stat. 339), accepted, ratified, and confirmed the Constitution adopted by a vote of the people of Alaska in an election held on April 24, 1956 and provided for the admission of the state of Alaska into the union on an equal footing with the other states of the union upon compliance with certain procedural requirements specified in that act; and

Whereas it appears from information before me that a majority of the legal votes cast at an election held on August 26, 1958, were in favor of each of the propositions required to be submitted to the people of Alaska by Section 8 (b) of the act of July 7, 1958; and

Whereas it further appears from information before me that a general election was held on November 25, 1958, and that the returns of the general election were made and certified as provided in the act of July 7, 1958; and

Whereas the acting governor of Alaska has certified to me the results of the submission to the people of Alaska of the three propositions set forth in Section 8 (b) of the act of July 7, 1958, and the results of the general election; and

Whereas I find and announce that the people of Alaska have duly adopted the propositions required to be submitted to them by the act of July 7, 1958, and have duly elected the officers required to be elected by that act;

Now, therefore, I, Dwight D. Eisenhower, President of the United States of America, do hereby declare and proclaim that the procedural requirements imposed by the Congress on the State of Alaska to entitle that state to admission into the union have been complied with in all respects and that admission of the State of Alaska into the union on an equal footing with the other states of the union is now accomplished.

In witness whereof, I have hereunto set my hand and caused the seal of the United States of America to be affixed.

Done at the city of Washington at one minute past noon on this

(Seal) Third day of January in the Year of our Lord nineteen hundred and fifty-nine and of the United States of America the one hundred and eighty-third.

Dwight D. Eisenhower

By the President:
Christian A. Herter,
Acting Secretary of State.

Missed Being First Baby

An eight-pound, three ounce word in Rogers Park was born today but missed being a state at 8:11 a.m. in Providence Hospital baby by just 42 minutes paid. If he had delayed his arrival... would have... The new son of Mr. and Mrs. James Black of West Spruce was a state at 8:11 a.m.

Review of the Week . . . . By Hafling

STATEHOOD FINAL TODAY

HELLO HAWAII! LET ME TELL YOU ABOUT MY OPERATION!

BEARD GROWERS TO REGISTER

NO MYRON — YOU'RE TOO BRISTLY AND YOU'RE NOT EVEN REGISTERED!

SLED DOG RACES UNDERWAY

OH HOW I HATE THESE SUNDAY DRIVERS!

LIARS ASK ALASKAN ENTRIES

BOY — THERE'S A NATURAL! JUST TELL THEM THAT STORY OF HOW YOU CAME IN SO LATE LAST NIGHT!

PINNING THE 49TH STAR

Seven-year-old Ann Herbert, daughter of Maj. and Mrs. James Herbert, pinned the 49th star on the American Flag today in a special ceremony at the Sydney Laurence Auditorium. C. Kip Huddleston,

president of the Anchorage Chamber of Commerce, holds the youngster as she pinned the star that marked the official entry of Alaska into the Union here.

Ike Unfurls New 49-Star Flag

WASHINGTON ⌐ — The supremacy of the federal government over state will continue to develop in the new flag, unfurled today, some will continue to develop, the President. Eisenhower said the new flag as long as it is a still have the usual 13 red and white stripes and 49 stars arranged along clusters of second flags are the staggered rows of 7 each exhausted. It is appropriate to alternate some of the stars are of primary to do the stars ordered.

The President, after employing Alaska the 49th state, signed an executive order fixing the new design for the United States flag.

By law, the order said, the new design has until Thru is a standard beside a standard banner cannot take effect until the official flag for the next July 4 the ceremonies.

"Display of the new flag before this time should by everyone be continued at the celebration — the order said. "This does of not recap the after July 4, 1959 and the citizens at will be improper to display means of the this after flag the whole that more than 500 "with limited exceptions suggestions.

EGAN IS SWORN IN AS FIRST STATE GOVERNOR

JUNEAU ⌐ — William A. Egan became the first governor of the newly created 49th state of Alaska today.

Egan, 41, a Democrat, took the oath of office at a brief ceremony in the capitol building here.

U.S. District Judge Raymond J. Kelly, a Republican and former national commander of the American Legion, administered the oath of office to Egan at 7:18 a.m. Pacific

Standard Time. (Anchorage time, 7:18 a.m.)

There was just beginning to break south at Juneau down the scenic Gastineau Channel, with the clear morning star visible from the windows of the governor's office where the oath was taken.

Hugh J. Wade, 60 Egan's running mate in Alaska's pre-statehood election in November, was sworn in two minutes later as secretary of state. The position corresponds to that of lieutenant governor in other states.

Two hours later, as bright sunshine bathed Juneau a snow a degree weather Egan took the wraps of a downtown theater and spoke briefly on the solemn meanings of statehood.

Egan, born 42 years ago in the Koola town of Valdez thrown his town operated a general store, said:

On this day a great gift has been granted us—self government.

The United States has made a state, as state can be — like all the world to see — that Uncle Sam practices what he preaches.

The responsibilities now is done. We have full number of freedom is. We have this great union of a governments.

This is a great occasion for Alaska. It represents a great and timely advance for the nation and the world with statehood at self government.

We accept the proud obligation of statehood and will seek to enhance the radiance of America's 49th star.

Across 1,000 typical mile many folks gathered in the theater for the brief statehood ceremony.

(Continued on Page 3)

Stroke Of President's Pen Makes It Official

By A. ROBERT SMITH
Times Washington Correspondent

WASHINGTON — Alaska is now a state.

President Eisenhower, surrounded by high officials of the government including Alaska's three-man congressional delegation, made it official a moment after the stroke of noon today by signing a proclamation which said:

"Admission of the State of Alaska into the union on an equal footing with the other states of the union is now accomplished."

The ceremony took place in the Cabinet room. The President took his high back black leather chair at the center of the table, placed House Speaker Sam Rayburn in a chair to his left and Vice President Nixon to his right.

Interior Secretary Fred Seaton stood just behind the President's chair. Fanned out to his right were senators-elect Bob Bartlett, just behind Nixon's chair, Ernest Gruening and Rep.-elect Ralph Rivers. To Seaton's left were Acting Territorial Gov. Waino Hendrickson, Ex-Gov. Mike Stepovich and Robert B. Atwood, chairman of the statehood committee.

They all huddled over the President's shoulders as he briskly picked up one after another of six pens placed before him and wrote "Dwight D. Eisenhower" at the bottom of the proclamation.

A battery of movie and TV cameras whirred furiously recording the historic event. Flash cameras banged away under the klieg lights set up in advance, standing room only crowd of newsmen and White House aides spilled out of the Cabinet room into the hallway.

Dignified Ceremony Marks Event

Alaskans in Anchorage and Alaskans in Washington, D.C., jointly observed the statehood proclamation today in a special telephone connection between the White House and the Sydney Laurence Auditorium here.

Mayor Hewitt Lounsbury, chief executive of the "largest city of the largest state in the union," accepted the call for Alaska here from Robert B. Atwood, chairman of the Alaska Statehood Committee, who was in the White House for the presidential proclamation.

The telephone call, tried to address system, included greetings and comments from other Alaskans in Washington: Sen. Former Governor Mike Stepovich, Acting Governor Waino Hendrickson, Senators-elect E.L. Bartlett and Ernest Gruening and Representatives-elect Ralph Rivers.

A large crowd of Alaskans packed the auditorium to participate in the special ceremony here in observance of President Eisenhower signing the proclamation that officially makes Alaska the 49th state.

Federal Judge J. L. McCarrey Jr., master of ceremonies, paid tribute to the early-day pioneers of Alaska, declaring:

"We gather here today to formally celebrate the achievement of a long, hard-fought battle which have initiated statehood for Alaska... This victory is one teeming with ideals and aspirations, and is one of the fruits and blessings principally limited to our prized American democracy."

The true pioneers and prospectors that came north to settle in Alaska had but one thought in mind

(Continued on Page 3)

Gov. Egan In Hospital

JUNEAU ⌐ — Gov. William A. Egan, sworn in today as chief executive of the 49th state, was admitted to St. Ann's Hospital here a few hours later.

His physician said the governor was suffering from a painful condition and would be in the hospital for several days for diagnosis.

Egan underwent an operation here Dec. 1 and had not fully recuperated at the time of his inauguration.

The previous operation was to correct a hemorrhoid condition. His doctor said the new ailment had no connection with the previous condition.

The doctor said it would be Tuesday before he could determine how soon Egan could undertake official duties.

TRAIN DERAILED

MONTREAL ⌐ — Thirteen cars of a Canadian National Railways passenger train were derailed today in the wilderness country about 300 miles north of Montreal.

(Continued on Page 3)

Text Of The President's Remarks

WASHINGTON — Following is the text of President Eisenhower's statement remarks at White House ceremonies today admitting Alaska as the 49th state:

Gentlemen I think that all of us together that as we foster arranged particularly for these I feel vary privileged and I am proud to welcome this forty-ninth state into the union.

The approximation now is done. We have full number of freedom is. We have this great union of freedom.

...

Alaska becomes a state.

competitive and exciting, and the fifty-five winners included housewives, lawyers, fishermen, and businessmen. With outside help and inside talent, Alaska drew up a model constitution, signed by the delegates, and the people voted to adopt it.

After party primaries, in October, 1956, the people elected two senators and one representative to go to the Congress in Washington to see if they would be accepted.

Every person in Alaska, from the oldest sourdough prospectors to the youngest Indian and Eskimo school children, waited and wondered. What a to-do! The national press, radio, and television, most of which supported the statehood drive, kept the world well informed. Nobody was overlooking Alaska now.

The men elected to represent Alaska in Congress left the Territory in special white automobiles with Benny Benson's blue and gold flag of Alaska painted on the doors. With signs proclaiming "Alaska, the 49th State," they drove down the Alcan Highway all the way to Washington, in time for the opening of Congress in January, 1957.

The Alaskans were in the gallery when Senator Spessard Holland of Florida asked the Congress to accept the Alaska delegation and to pass the law to admit Alaska as a state. In spite of the waves of applause, it was June 30, 1958, many debates later, before the Congress finally voted to admit Alaska to the Union.

In Alaska the people went wild when the news was received at mid-afternoon that June day. In Fairbanks all the bells and sirens in town rang or blew for five solid minutes. Guns and firecrackers and shouts resounded throughout the new state. President Dwight Eisenhower signed the bill on July 7, and on August 26, 1958, most of the over 200,000 Alaskans went to the polls and voted to accept the terms of the statehood bill.

At last, on January 3, 1959, Alaska was formally admitted as the forty-ninth state, and a new American flag with forty-nine stars was unfurled at the Capitol.

It hadn't been easy to become a state.

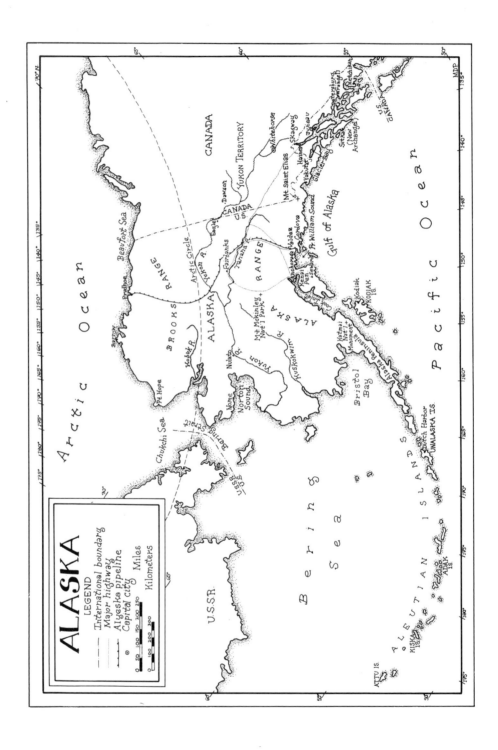

22 ❖❖❖

Pipelines and Politics

ALMOST everybody has heard of Alaska's oil and the big pipeline that was built in the 1970's to carry that oil from the Arctic Ocean to the Pacific Ocean.

In 1967 so much oil was discovered at Prudhoe Bay that corporations fought to get leases to drill and sell it. In 1969 the State of Alaska sold $900,000,000 worth of oil and gas rights to corporations. The Eskimos, Aleuts, and Indians, Alaska's first people, had been raising their voices about their rights to their ancient land.

"This land is ours," many of them said. "Our people were here first, long before the Russians or the Americans came. This land has been taken from us, and as American citizens, we object!"

One outspoken young Eskimo, Charles "Etok" Edwardsen, Jr., went to Washington and shouted his protests to Congress. Congressmen knew little about the Native Americans in the faraway state of Alaska, but they listened. The Native people and their supporters were so determined that their traditional hunting and fishing lands should not be taken from them that government officials said, "Hold it! There will be no more sales or leases or land transfers until the Native land claims are settled."

Oil executives fumed in their air-conditioned offices, for this meant that no pipeline could be built to carry out the profitable oil until the

Eskimo camp, Point Hope

Native claims were settled by Congress. Eskimos and Indians in their summer hunting and fishing tents or their small village winter dwellings met in angry groups, discussing the situation and organizing for action.

The most unlikely set of partners that could be imagined, the oil people and Alaska Natives, were working for the same end. The Native people wanted their land assured to them for their own use, and the oil people wanted the Native rights settled so they could begin pumping and piping oil. So the oil people put mighty pressure on Congress to settle the Native land claims, using the kind of power that the Native people might never have managed alone.

Congress acted in a hurry and passed a law, the Alaska Native Claims Settlement Act. The Natives of Alaska, descendants of Stone Age migrants from Asia, were organized into twelve regional corporations. All United States citizens with one-fourth or more Alaska Indian, Eskimo, or Aleut blood who were living when the law passed in 1971 were made members of a corporation. Over forty million acres of land and nearly ten million

**Views of the
Alyeska pipeline**

Beautiful Alaska

dollars would be paid to the corporations. This was the biggest Native claims settlement the world had ever seen.

And now the way was cleared for the building of the controversial pipeline. Many American environmentalists, including Alaska Natives, objected vigorously to opening up the wild interior of Alaska. As a consequence, many safeguards for the animals and land were required of the pipeline builders.

Skilled and unskilled workers, women and men, came to Alaska to work in the killing cold of winter, the grinding heat of summer amidst the stings of man-eating mosquitoes, to complete the ten-billion-dollar Alyeska pipeline from Prudhoe Bay to Valdez. Hard work and wicked weather were nothing new to Alaska.

In a boom as big as all the gold rushes combined, the pipeline was finally finished, and oil ran through it to be delivered to waiting tankers in the summer of 1977.

Was it all worth it? Did America need the oil? Were the animals and the land and the Native peoples helped or hurt by it all? Probably only Raven knows—and who can understand what he is saying as he flaps around the oil rigs spouting his opinions?

Index

About The Author

Cora Cheney says of herself: "When I was a child my aunt made a trip to Alaska. Her stories of half a century ago gave me such an early dose of Alaska fever that I had to go follow them up and bring them up to date."

It was only recently that Cora Cheney realized her childhood ambition to investigate our forty-ninth state.

With her husband, Ben Partridge, she saw Alaska from Juneau to Prudhoe, from Chicken to Nome, from St. Lawrence Island to the Arctic coast, as well as the interior. She spent months doing original research at the Alaska State Historical Library and the Alaska State Museum to find the binding background of the tales she has woven into a chronological collection that should appeal to all ages. Especially intriguing are the stories of Russian Alaska.

Cora Cheney has written many books of adventure, history, and folklore. She and her husband live on a farm at South Windham, Vermont, when they are not cruising on their sloop *Iglu*.